THE AGE OF ERASMUS

THE AGE OF ERASMUS

LECTURES DELIVERED IN THE UNIVERSITIES OF OXFORD AND LONDON

BY

P. S. ALLEN, M.A.

FELLOW OF MERTON COLLEGE, OXFORD

Wipf & Stock
PUBLISHERS
Eugene, Oregon

Wipf and Stock Publishers
199 W 8th Ave, Suite 3
Eugene, OR 97401

The Age of Erasmus
Lectures Delivered in the Universities of Oxford and London
By Allen, P.S.
ISBN: 1-57910-084-8
Publication date 11/12/1997

CONTENTS

I

THE ADWERT ACADEMY

THE importance of biography for the study of history can hardly be overrated. In a sense it is true that history should be like the law and 'care not about very small things'; concerning itself not so much with individual personality as with fundamental causes affecting the rise and fall of nations or the development of mental outlook from one age to another. But even if this be conceded, we still must not forget that the course of history is worked out by individuals, who, in spite of the accidental condensation that the needs of human life thrust upon them, are isolated at the last and alone—for no man may deliver his brother. In consequence, it is only in periods when the stream of personal record flows wide and deep that history begins to live, and that we have a chance to view it through the eyes of the actors instead of projecting upon it our own fancies and conceptions.

One of the features that makes the study of the Renaissance so fascinating is that in that age the stream of personal record, which had been driven underground, its course choked and hidden beneath the fallen masonry of the Roman Empire, emerges again unimpeded and flows in ever-increasing volume. For reconstruction of the past we are no longer limited to charters and institutions, or the mighty works of men's hands. In place of a mental output, rigidly confined within unbending modes of thought and expression, we have a literature that reflects the varied phases of human life, that can discard romance and look upon the commonplace; and instead of dry and meagre chronicles, rarely producing evidence at first hand, we have rich store of memoirs and private letters, by means of which we can form real pictures of individuals—approaching almost to personal acquaintance and intimacy—and regard the same events from many points of view, to perception of the circumstances that 'alter cases'.

The period of the Transalpine Renaissance corresponds roughly with the life of Erasmus (1466–1536); from the days when Northern scholars began to win fame for themselves in reborn Italy, until the width of the humanistic outlook was narrowed and the progress of the reawakened studies overwhelmed by the tornado of the Reformation. The aim of these lectures is not so much to draw the outlines of the Renaissance in the North as to present sketches of the world through which Erasmus passed, and to view it as it appeared to him and to some of his contemporaries, famous or obscure. And firstly of the generation that preceded him in the wide but undefined region known then as Germany.

The Cistercian Abbey of Adwert near Groningen, under the enlightened governance of Henry of Rees

(1449–85), was a centre to which were attracted most of the scholars whose names are famous in the history of Northern humanism in the second half of the fifteenth century: Wessel, Agricola, Hegius, Langen, Vrye, and others. They came on return from visits to Italy or the universities; men of affairs after discharge of their missions; schoolmasters to rest on their holidays; parish priests in quest of change: all found a welcome from the hospitable Abbot, and their talk ranged far and wide, over the pursuit of learning, till Adwert merited the name of an 'Academy'.

Earliest of these is John Wessel († 1489), and perhaps also the most notable; certainly the others looked up to him with a veneration which seems to transcend the natural pre-eminence of seniority. Unfortunately the details of his life have not been fully established. Thirty years after his death, when it was too late for him to define his own views, the Reformers claimed him for their own; and in consequence his body has been wrangled over with the heat which seeks not truth but victory. His father, Hermann Wessel, was a baker from the Westphalian village of Gansfort or Goesevort, who settled in Groningen. After some years in the town school, the boy was about to be apprenticed to a trade, as his parents were too poor to help him further; but the good Oda Jargis, hearing how well he had done at his books, sent him to the school at Zwolle, in which the Brethren of the Common Life took part. There, as at Groningen, he rose to the top, and in his last years, as a first-form boy, also did some teaching in the third form, according to the custom of the school. He came into contact with Thomas à Kempis, who was then at the monastery of Mount St. Agnes, half an hour outside Zwolle, and was profoundly influenced by him. The course at Zwolle lasted eight years, and there is reason to suppose that he completed it in full. He was lodged in the Parua Domus, a hostel for fifty boys, and we are told that he and his next neighbour made a hole through the wall which divided their rooms—probably only a wooden partition—and taught one another: Wessel imparting earthly wisdom, and receiving in exchange the fear and love of the Lord. In the autumn of 1449 he matriculated at Cologne, entering the Bursa Laurentiana; in December 1450 he was B.A., and in February 1452, M.A.

By 1455 he had arrived at Paris and entered upon his studies for the theological degree. Within a year he conceived a profound distaste for the philosophy dominant in the schools; and though he persevered for some time, his frequent dissension from his teachers earned for him the title of 'Magister contradictionis'. After this his movements cannot be traced until 1470, when he was at Rome in the train of Cardinal Francesco della Rovere. In the interval he studied medicine, and, if report be true, travelled far; venturing into the East, just when the fall of Constantinople had turned the tide of Hellenism westward. In Greece he read Aristotle in the original, and learnt to prefer Plato; in Egypt he sought in vain for the books of Solomon and a mythical library of Hebrew treasures.

In 1471 his Cardinal-patron was elected Pope as Sixtus IV. The magnificence which characterized the poor peasant's son in his dealings with Italy, in his embellishment of Rome and the Vatican, was not lacking in his treatment of Wessel. 'Ask what you please as a parting gift', he said to the scholar, who was preparing to set out for Friesland. 'Give me books from your library, Greek and Hebrew', was the request. 'What? No benefice, no grant of office or fees? Why not?' 'Because I don't want them', came the quiet reply. The books were forthcoming—one, a Greek Gospels, was perhaps the parent of a copy which reached Erasmus for the second edition of his New Testament.

After his return to the North, Wessel was invited to Heidelberg, to aid the Elector Palatine, Philip, in restoring the University, *c.* 1477. He was without the degree in theology which would have enabled him to teach in that faculty, and was not even in orders: indeed a proposal that he should qualify by entering the lowest grade and receiving the tonsure, he contemptuously rejected. So the Theological Faculty would not hear him, but to the students in Arts he lectured on Greek and Hebrew and philosophy. For some years, too, he was physician to David of Burgundy, Bishop of Utrecht, whom he cured of gout by making him take baths of warm milk. The Bishop rewarded him by shielding him from the attacks of the Dominicans, who were incensed by his bold criticisms of Aquinas; and when age brought the desire for rest, the Bishop set him over a house of nuns at Groningen, and bought him the right to visit Mount St. Agnes whenever he liked, by paying for the board and lodging of this welcome guest.

Wessel's last years were happily spent. He was the acknowledged leader of his society, and he divided his time between Mount St. Agnes and the sisters at Groningen, with occasional visits to Adwert. There he set about reviving the Abbey schools, one elementary, within its walls, the other more advanced, in a village near by; and Abbot Rees warmly supported him. Would-be pupils besought him to teach them Greek and Hebrew. Admiring friends came to hear him talk, and brought their sons to see this glory of their country—Lux mundi, as he was called. Some fragments of his conversation have been preserved, the unquestioned judgements which his hearers loyally received. Of the Schoolmen he was contemptuous, with their honorific titles: 'doctor angelic, doctor seraphic, doctor subtle, doctor irrefragable.' 'Was Thomas ⟨Aquinas⟩ a doctor? So am I. Thomas scarcely knew Latin, and that was his only tongue: I have a fair knowledge of the three languages. Thomas saw Aristotle only as a phantom: I have read him in Greece in his own words.' To Ostendorp, then a young man, but afterwards to become head master of Deventer school, he gave the counsel: 'Read the ancients, sacred and profane: modern doctors, with their robes and distinctions, will soon be drummed out of town.' At Mount St. Agnes once he was asked why he never used rosary nor book of hours. 'I try', he replied, 'to pray always. I say the Lord's Prayer once every day. Said once a year in the right spirit it would have more weight than all these vain repetitions.'

He loved to read aloud to the brethren on Sunday evenings; his favourite passage being John xiii–xviii, the discourse at the Last Supper. As he grew older, he sometimes stumbled over his words. He was not an imposing figure, with his eyes somewhat a-squint and his slight limp; and sometimes the younger monks fell into a titter, irreverent souls, to hear him so eager in his reading and so unconscious. It was not his eyesight that was at fault: to the end he could read the smallest hand without any glasses, like his great namesake, John Wesley, whom a German traveller noticed on the packet-boat between Flushing and London reading the fine print of the Elzevir Virgil, with his eyes unaided, though at an advanced age.

On his death-bed Wessel was assailed with scepticism, and began to doubt about the truth of the Christian religion. But the cloud was of short duration. That supreme moment of revelation, which comes to every man once, is no time for fear. Patient hope cast out questioning, and he passed through the deep waters with his eyes on the Cross which had been his guide through the life that was ending.

Of Rudolph Agricola we know more than of the others; his striking personality, it seems, moved many of his friends to put on record their impressions of him. One of the best of these sketches is by Goswin of Halen († 1530), who had been Wessel's servant at Groningen, and had frequently met Agricola. Rudolph's father, Henry Huusman, was the parish priest of Baflo, a village four hours to the north of Groningen; his mother being a young woman of the place, who subsequently married a local carrier. On 17 Feb. 1444 the priest was elected to be warden of a college of nuns at Siloe, close to Groningen, and in the same hour a messenger came running to him from Baflo, claiming the reward of good news and announcing the birth of a son. 'Good,' said the new warden; 'this is an auspicious day, for it has twice made me father.'

From the moment he could walk, the boy was passionately fond of music; the sound of church bells would bring him toddling out into the street, or the thrummings of the blind beggars as they went from house to house playing for alms; and he would follow strolling pipers out of the gates into the country, and only be driven back by a show of violence. When he was taken to church, all through the mass his eyes were riveted upon the organ and its bellows; and as he grew older he made himself a syrinx with eight or nine pipes out of willow-bark. He was taught to ride on horseback, and early became adept in pole-jumping whilst in the saddle, an art which the Frieslanders of that age had evolved to help their horses across the broad rhines of their country. In 1456, when he was just 12, he matriculated at Erfurt, and in May 1462 at Cologne. But the course of his education is not clear, and though it is known that he reached the M.A. at Louvain, the date of this degree is not certain. He is also said to have been at the University of Paris.

Of his life at Louvain some details are given by Geldenhauer († 1542) in a sketch written about fifty years after Agricola's death. The University had been founded in 1426 to meet the needs of Belgian students, who for higher education had been obliged to go to Cologne or Paris, or more distant universities. Agricola entered Kettle College, which afterwards became the college of the Falcon, and soon distinguished himself among his fellow-students. They admired the ease with which he learnt French —not the rough dialect of Hainault, but the polite language of the court. With many his musical tastes were a bond of sympathy, in a way which recalls the evenings that Henry Bradshaw used to spend among the musical societies of Bruges and Lille when he was working in Belgian libraries; and on all sides men frankly acknowledged his intellectual pre-eminence as they marked his quiet readiness in debate and heard him pose the lecturers with acute questions. By nature he was silent and absorbed, and often in company he would sit deaf to all questions, his elbows on the table and biting his nails. But when roused he was at once captivating; and this unintended rudeness never lost him a friend. There was a small band of true humanists, who, as Geldenhauer puts it, 'had begun to love purity of Latin style'; to them he was insensibly attracted, and spent with them over Cicero and Quintilian hours filched from the study of Aristotle. Later in life he openly regretted having spent as much as seven years over the scholastic philosophy, which he had learnt to regard as profitless.

From 1468 to 1479 he was for the most part in Italy, except for occasional visits to the North, when we see him staying with his father at Siloe, and, in 1474, teaching Greek to Hegius at Emmerich. Many positions were offered to him already; gifts such as his have not to stand waiting in the market-place. But his wits were not homely, and the world called him. Before he could settle he must see many men and many cities, and learn what Italy had to teach him.

For the first part of his time there, until 1473, he was at Pavia studying law and rhetoric; but on his return from home in 1474 he went to Ferrara in order to enjoy the better opportunities for learning Greek afforded by the court of Duke Hercules of Este and its circle of learned men. His description of the place is interesting: 'The town is beautiful, and so are the women. The University has not so many faculties as Pavia, nor are they so well attended; but *literae humaniores* seem to be in the very air. Indeed, Ferrara is the home of the

Muses—and of Venus.' One special delight to him was that the Duke had a fine organ, and he was able to indulge what he describes as his 'old weakness for the organs'. In October 1476, at the opening of the winter term of the University, the customary oration before the Duke was delivered by Rodolphus Agricola Phrysius. His eloquence surprised the Italians, coming from so outlandish a person: 'a Phrygian, I believe', said one to another, with a contemptuous shrug of the shoulders. But Agricola, with his chestnut-brown hair and blue eyes, was no Oriental; only a Frieslander from the North, whose cold climate to the superb Italians seemed as benumbing to the intellect as we consider that of the Esquimaux.

During this period Agricola translated Isocrates *ad Demonicum* and the *Axiochus de contemnenda morte*, a dialogue wrongly attributed to Plato, which was a favourite in Renaissance days. Also he completed the chief composition of his lifetime, the *De inuentione dialectica*, a considerable treatise on rhetoric. His favourite books, Geldenhauer tells us, were Pliny's Natural History, the younger Pliny's Letters, Quintilian's *Institutio Oratoria*, and selections from Cicero and Plato. These were his travelling library, carried with him wherever he went; two of them, Pliny's Letters and Quintilian, he had copied out with his own hand. Other books, as he acquired them, he planted out in friends' houses as pledges of return.

In 1479 he left Italy and went home. On his

way he stayed for some months with the Bishop of Augsburg at Dillingen, on the Danube, and there translated Lucian's *De non facile credendis delationibus*. A manuscript of Homer sorely tempted him to stay on through the winter. He felt that without Homer his knowledge of Greek was incomplete; and he proposed to copy it out from beginning to end, or at any rate the Iliad. But home called him, and he went on. At Spires, in quest of manuscripts, he went with a friend to the cathedral library. He describes it as not bad for Germany, though it contained nothing in Greek, and only a few Latin manuscripts of any interest—a Livy and a Pliny, very old, but much injured and the texts corrupt—and nothing at all that could be called eloquence, that is to say, pure literature.

When he had been a little while in Groningen, the town council bethought them to turn his talents and learning to some account. He was a fine figure of a man, who would make a creditable show in conducting their business; and for composing the elegant Latin epistles, which every respectable corporation felt bound to rise to on occasions, no one was better equipped than he. He was retained as town secretary, and in the four years of his service went on frequent embassies. During the first year we hear of him visiting his father at Siloe, and contracting a friendship with one of the nuns [1];

[1] In view of Geldenhauer's testimony to Agricola's high character in this respect, we need not question, as does Goswin of Halen, the nature of this intimacy.

to whom he afterwards sent a work of Eucherius, bishop of Lyons, which he had found in a manuscript at Roermond. Twice he visited Brussels on embassy to Maximilian; and in the next year he followed the Archduke's court for several months, visiting Antwerp, and making the acquaintance of Barbiriau, the famous musician. Maximilian offered him the post of tutor to his children and Latin secretary to himself; the town of Antwerp invited him to become head of their school. He might easily have accepted. He was not altogether happy at Groningen. His countrymen had done him honour, but they had no real appreciation for learning, and some of them were boorish and cross-grained. It was the old story of Pegasus in harness; the practical men of business and the scholar impatient of restraint. His parents, too, were now both dead—in 1480, within a few months of each other—and such homes as he had had, with his father amongst the nuns at Siloe and with his mother in the house of her husband the tranter, were therefore closed to him. And yet neither invitation attracted him. Friesland was his native land; and for all his wanderings the love of it was in his blood. Adwert, too, was near, and Wessel. He refused, and stayed on in his irksome service.

But in 1482 came an offer he could not resist. An old friend of Pavia days, John of Dalberg, for whom he had written the oration customary on his installation as Rector in 1474, had just been appointed Bishop of Worms. He invited Agricola for a visit, and urged him to come and join him; living partly as a friend in the Bishop's household, partly lecturing at the neighbouring University of Heidelberg. The opening was just such as Agricola wished, and he eagerly accepted; but circumstances at Groningen prevented him from redeeming his promise until the spring of 1484. For little more than a year he rejoiced in the new position, which gave full scope for his abilities. Then he set out to Rome with Dalberg, their business being to deliver the usual oration of congratulation to Innocent VIII on his election. On the way back he fell ill of a fever at Trent, and the Bishop had to leave him behind. He recovered enough to struggle back to Heidelberg, but only to die in Dalberg's arms on 27 Oct. 1485, at the age of 41.

Few men of letters have made more impression on their contemporaries; and yet his published writings are scanty. The generation that followed sought for his manuscripts as though they were of the classics; but thirty years elapsed before the *De inuentione dialectica* was printed, and more than fifty before there was a collected edition. Besides his letters the only thing which has permanent value is a short educational treatise, *De formando studio*, which he wrote in 1484, and addressed to Barbiriau—some compensation to the men of Antwerp for his refusal to come to them. His work was to learn and to teach rather than to write. To learn Greek when few others were learning it, and when the apparatus of grammar and dictionary had to be made by the student for himself, was a task to consume even abundant energies; and still more so, if Hebrew, too, was to be acquired. But though he left little, the fire of his enthusiasm did not perish with him; passing on by tradition, it kindled in others whom he had not known, the flame of interest in the wisdom of the ancients.

Another member of the Adwert gatherings was Alexander of Heek in Westphalia, hence called Hegius (1433–98). He was an older man than Agricola, but was not ashamed to learn of him when an opportunity offered to acquire Greek. His enthusiasm was for teaching; and to that he gave his life, first at Wesel, then at Emmerich, and finally for fifteen years at Deventer, where he had many eminent humanists under his care—Erasmus, William Herman, Mutianus Rufus, Hermann Busch, John Faber, John Murmell, Gerard Geldenhauer. Butzbach, who was the last pupil he admitted, and who saw him buried in St. Lebuin's church on a winter's evening at sunset, describes him at great length; and besides his learning and simplicity, praises the liberality with which he gave all that he had to help the needy: living in the house of another (probably Richard Paffraet, the printer) and sharing expenses, and leaving at his death no possessions but his books and a few clothes. And yet he was master of a school which had over 2000 boys.

Rudolph Langen of Munster (1438–1519) was another who was known at Adwert. He matriculated at Erfurt in the same year as Agricola, and was M.A. there in 1460. A canonry at Munster gave him maintenance for his life, and he devoted his energies to learning. Twice he visited Italy, in 1465 and 1486; and in 1498 he succeeded in establishing a school at Munster on humanistic lines, and wished Hegius to become head master, but in vain. Nevertheless it rapidly rivalled the fame of Deventer.

Finally, Antony Vrye (Liber) of Soest deserves record, since he has contributed somewhat to our knowledge of Adwert. He also was a schoolmaster, and taught at various times at Emmerich, Campen, Amsterdam, and Alcmar. In 1477 he published a volume entitled *Familiarium Epistolarum Compendium*, the composition of which illustrates the catholic tastes of the humanists; for it contains selections from the letters of Cicero, Jerome, Symmachus, and the writers of the Italian Renaissance. But he chiefly merits our gratitude for including in the book a number of letters which passed between the visitors to Adwert and their friends, together with some of his own. The pleasant relations existing in this little society may be illustrated by the fact that when Vrye's son John had reached student age, the Adwert friends subscribed to pay his expenses at a university; and thus secured him an education which enabled him to become Syndic of Campen.

A few extracts from their letters will serve to show some of the characteristics of the age, its wide interest in the past, theological as well as classical; its eager search for manuscripts, and the freedom with which its libraries were opened; its concern for education, and its attitude towards the old learning; and the extent of its actual achievements. The earliest of these letters that survive are a series written by Langen from Adwert in the spring of 1469 to Vrye at Soest. Despite the grave interest in serious study that the letters show, there are human touches about them. One begins: 'You promised faithfully to return, and yet you have not come. But I cannot blame you; for the road is deep in mud, and I myself too am so feeble a walker that I can imagine the weariness of others' feet.' Another ends in haste, not with the departure of the post, but 'The servants are waiting to conduct me to bed'. Here is a longer sample:

1. LANGEN TO VRYE: from Adwert, 27 Feb. ⟨1469⟩.

'Why do you delay so long to gratify the wishes of our devout friend Wolter? With my own hand I have transcribed the little book of *Elegantiae,* as far as the section about the reckoning of the Kalends. I greatly desire to have this precious work complete; so do send me the portion we lack as soon as you can. The little book will be my constant companion: I know nothing that has such value in so narrow a span. How brilliant Valla is! he has raised up Latin to glory from the bondage of the barbarians. May the earth lie lightly on him and the spring shine ever round his urn! Even if the book is not by Valla himself, it must come from his school.

'I write in haste and with people talking all round me, from whom politeness will not let me sit altogether aloof. But read carefully and you will understand me. At least I hope this letter won't be quite so barbarous as the monstrosities which the usher from Osnabruck sends you every day: they sound like the spells of witches to bring up their familiar spirits, or the enchantments "Fecana kageti", &c., which open locks whoever knocks. Poor Latin! it is worse handled than was Regulus by the Carthaginians. Forgive this scrawl: I am writing by candlelight.'

We shall have other occasions to notice the admiration of the Northern humanists for Lorenzo Valla († 1457), the master of Latin style, and the audacious Canon of the Lateran, who could apply the spirit of criticism not only to the New Testament but even to the Donation of Constantine.

2. Vrye to Arnold of Hildesheim (Schoolmaster at Emmerich): ⟨? Cologne, *c.* 1477⟩.

'I have still a great many things to do, but I shall not begin upon them till the printed books from Cologne arrive at Deventer. My plan was to go to Heidelberg, Freiburg, Basle and some of the universities in the East and then return to Deventer through Saxony and Westphalia. But at Coblenz I met four men from Strasburg who declared that Upper Germany was almost all overrun by soldiers. This unexpected alarm has compelled me to dispose of the 1500 copies of *The Revival of Latin* amongst the schools.[1] After visiting Deventer and Zwolle I shall go to Louvain, and then, if it is safe, to Paris. I thought you ought to know of this change in my plans; that you might not be taken by surprise at finding me gone westwards instead of into Upper Germany.

'Please take great pains over the correction of the manuscripts.'

3. AGRICOLA TO HEGIUS ⟨at Emmerich⟩: from Groningen, 20 Sept. 1480.

'I was very sorry to learn from your letter that you had been here just when I was away. There are so few opportunities of meeting any one who cares for learning that you would have been most welcome. My position becomes increasingly distasteful to me: since I left Italy, I forget everything—the classics, history, even how to write with any style. In prose I can get neither ideas nor language. Such as come only serve to fill the page with awkward, disjointed sentences. Verse I hardly ever attempt, and when I do, there is no flow about it; sometimes the lines almost refuse to scan. The fact is that I can find no one here who is interested in these things. If only we were together!

'My youngest brother Henry has been fired with the desire to study. I have advised him against it, but as he persists, I do not like to do more. For the last six months he has been with Frederic Mormann at Munster, and has made some progress: but now

[1] particularibus studiis.

Mormann ⟨who was one of the Brethren of the Common Life⟩ has been sent as Rector to a house ⟨at Marburg⟩, and Henry has come home. If you can have him, I should like him to come to you. He will bring with him the usual furniture,[1] money will be sent to him from time to time, and he will find himself a lodging[2] wherever you advise. I should be glad to know whether there are any teachers who give lessons out of school hours, as Mormann does; and whether any one may go to them on payment of a fee, whether candidates for orders[3] or not. I should like him to get over the elements as quickly as possible; for if boys are kept at them too long, they take a dislike to the whole thing. The Pliny that you ask for shall come to you soon. I use it a great deal; but nevertheless you shall have it.'

In answer to a question from Hegius, Agricola goes on to distinguish the words mimus, histrio, persona, scurra, nebulo; with quotations from Juvenal and Gellius. 'Leccator', he says, 'is a German word; like several others that we have turned into bad Latin, reisa, burgimagister, scultetus, or like the French passagium for a military expedition, guerra for war, treuga for truce.'

He then proceeds to more derivations in answer

[1] victui necessaria, vt solent nostrates. Victus is commonly used in the technical sense of 'board'; but here the meaning probably is 'the usual outfit for a schoolboy'. Gebwiler, in 1530, required a boy coming to his school at Hagenau to be provided with 'a bed, sheets, pillow, and other necessaries'.

[2] diuersorium. [3] capitiati.

to Hegius. Ἄνθρωπος he considers a fundamental word, which, like homo, defies analysis: but nevertheless he suggests ἀνά and τρέπω, or τέρπω, or τρέφω. To explain vesper he cites Sallust, Catullus, Ovid, Pliny's Letters, Caesar's Civil War, Persius and Suetonius. (We must remember that in those days a man's quotations were culled from his memory, not from a dictionary or concordance.) He goes on: 'About forming words by analogy, I rarely allow myself to invent words which are not in the best authors, but still perhaps I might use Socratitas, Platonitas, entitas, though Valla I am sure would object. After all one must be free, when there is necessity. Cicero, without any need, used Pietas and Lentulitas; and Pollio talks of Livy's Patauinitas.' Other words explained are tignum, asser, διοίκησις; and then Agricola proceeds to correct a number of mistakes in Hegius' letter. Rather delicate work it might seem; but there is such good humour between them that, though the corrections extend to some length, it all ends pleasantly.

4. HEGIUS TO AGRICOLA; from Deventer, 17 Dec. ⟨1484⟩.

After apologies for not having written for a long while, he proceeds:

'You ask how my school is doing. Well, it is full again now; but in summer the numbers rather fell off. The plague which killed twenty of the boys, drove many others away, and doubtless kept some from coming to us at all.

'Thank you for translating Lucian's Micyllus. I am sure that all of us who read it, will be greatly pleased with it. As soon as it comes, I will have it printed. If I may, I should much like to ask you for an abridgement of your book on Dialectic: it would be very valuable to students. I understand that you have translated Isocrates' Education of Princes. If I had it here, I would expound it to my pupils. For some of them, no doubt, will be princes some day and have to govern.

'I have been reading Valla's book on the True Good, and have become quite an Epicurean, estimating all things in terms of pleasure. Also it has persuaded me that each virtue has its contrary vice, rather than two vices as its extremes. I should like to know whether the authorities at Heidelberg have abandoned their Marsilius [1] on the question of universals, or whether they still stick to him.'

5. AGRICOLA TO HEGIUS; from Worms, Tuesday ⟨January 1485⟩, in reply.

After thanks and personalities he writes:

'Certainly you shall have the Lucian, and I will dedicate it to you: but not just yet, as I am too busy to revise it. My public lectures take up a good deal of my time. I have a fairly large audience; but their zeal is greater than their ability. The majority of them are M.A.'s or students in the Arts course; [2] who are obliged to spend all their

[1] Of Inghen, first Rector of Heidelberg University (1386), the author of the *Parua Logicalia*.

[2] Scholastici, vt nos dicimus, artium.

time on their disputations, so they have only a meagre part of the day left for these studies. In consequence, as they can do so little, I am not very active.

'In addition to this I am trying to keep up my Latin and Greek (though they are fast slipping from me) and am beginning Hebrew, which I find very difficult: indeed to my surprise it costs me more effort than Greek did. However, I shall go on with it as I have begun: also because I like to have something new on hand, and much as I like Greek, its novelty has somewhat worn off. I have made up my mind to devote my old age, if I ever reach it, to theology. You know how I detest the barbarisms of those who fill the schools. On their side they are indignant with me for daring to question their decisions; but this will not deter me.

'My greetings to your host, Master Richard ⟨Paffraet⟩, and his wife.

'Worms, in great haste, on the third day of the week: as I have determined to call it, instead of our unclassical Feria secunda, tertia, &c., or the heathen names, Monday, Mars' day, Mercury's day, Jove's day.'

We may notice the anticipation of the Quakers, who in a similar way would only speak of first day and sixth month.

6. Hegius to Wessel; from Deventer ⟨between 1483 and 1489⟩.

'I am sending you the Homilies of John Chrysostom, and hope you will enjoy reading them. His golden words have always been more acceptable to you than the precious metal itself from the mint.

'I have been, as you know, at Cusanus' library, and found there many Hebrew books which were quite unknown to me; also a few Greek. I remember the names of the following: Epiphanius against heresies, a very big book; Dionysius on the Hierarchy; Athanasius against Arius; Climacus.

'These I left behind there, but I brought away with me: Basil on the Hexaëmeron and some of his homilies on the Psalms; the Epistles of Paul and the Acts of the Apostles; Plutarch's Lives of Romans and Greeks, and his Symposium; some writings on grammar and mathematics; some poems on the Christian religion, written, I think, by Gregory Nazianzen; some prayers, in Latin and Greek.

'If there are any of these you lack, let me know and they shall come to you: for everything I have is at your disposal. If you could spare the Gospels in Greek, I should be grateful for the loan of it. You enquire what books we are using in the school. I have followed your advice; for literature which is dangerous to morality is most injurious.'

The library mentioned above was that of Nicholas Krebs († 1464), the famous Cardinal who took part in the Council of Basle and was the patron of Poggio. Cues on the Moselle was his birthplace, and gave him his name Cusanus. In his later years he founded a hostel, the Bursa Cusana, at Deventer, where he had been at school, and at Cues built a hospital for aged men and women, with a grassy quadrangle and a chapel of delicate Gothic; and there in a vaulted chamber supported by a central column he deposited the manuscripts, mainly theological but with some admixture of the classics, which he had gathered in the course of his busy life.

In 1496 we hear of another visit to it; when Dalberg, who was a prince of humanists, led thither Reuchlin and a party of friends on a voyage of discovery. Their course was from Worms to Oppenheim, where his mother was still living: by boat to Coblenz and up the Moselle to Cues: then over the hills to Dalburg, his ancestral home, and finally to the abbey of Sponheim, near Kreuznach, where they admired the rich collection of manuscripts in five languages formed by the learned historian Trithemius, who was then Abbot. Whether this gay party of pleasure also carried off any treasures from Cues is not recorded.

But lest this view of the Adwert Academy should appear too uniformly roseate, we will turn to the tradition of Reyner Praedinius (1510–59), who was Rector of the town school at Groningen, and whose fame attracted students thither from Italy, Spain, and Poland. He had in his possession several manuscripts of Wessel's writings, some of them unpublished; and he had been intimate with men who had known both Wessel and Agricola. One of these—very likely Goswin of Halen—as a boy had often served at table, when the two scholars were dining; and had afterwards shown them the way home with a lantern. He used to say that he had frequently pulled off Agricola's boots, when he came home the worse for his potations; but that no one had ever seen Wessel under the influence of wine. Wessel, indeed, lived to a green old age, but killed himself by working too hard.

II

SCHOOLS

Erasmus was born at Rotterdam on the vigil of SS. Simon and Jude, 27 October: probably in 1466, but his utterances on the subject are ambiguous. Around his parentage he wove a web of romance, from which only one fact emerges clearly—that his father was at some time a priest. Current gossip said that he was parish priest of Gouda; a little town near Rotterdam, with a big church, which in the sixteenth century its inhabitants were wealthy enough to adorn with some fine stained glass. There in the town school, under a master who was afterwards one of the guardians of his scanty patrimony, Erasmus' schooldays began, and he made acquaintance with the Latin grammar of Donatus. After an interval as chorister at Utrecht, he was sent by his parents to the school at Deventer, which, with that of the neighbouring and rival town of Zwolle, enjoyed pre-eminence among the schools of the Netherlands at that date. It was connected with the principal church of the town, St. Lebuin's; and doubtless among those aisles and chapels, listening perhaps to the merry bells, whose chimes still proclaim the quarters far and wide, he caught the first breath of that new hope to which he was to devote his whole life. The school was controlled by the canons of St. Lebuin, who appointed the head master; but, as at Zwolle, some of the teachers were drawn from that sober and learned order, the Brethren of the Common Life, whose parent house was at Deventer.

Of Erasmus' life in the school we have little knowledge. He tells us that he was there in 1475, when preachers came from Rome announcing the jubilee which Sixtus IV had so conveniently found possible to hold after only twenty-five years. From one of his letters we can picture him wandering by the river side among the barges, and marking the slow growth of the bridge of boats which it took the town of Deventer several years to throw across the rapid Yssel. He probably entered the lowest class, the eighth, and by 1484, when at the age of eighteen he left in consequence of the outbreak of plague mentioned in Hegius' letter to Agricola, he had not made his way above the third; thus giving little indication of his future fame. An explanation may perhaps be found by supposing that his time in the choir at Utrecht was an interlude in the Deventer period; but in any case the school in his time was still 'barbarous', to use his own word, that is, it was still modelled on the requirements of the scholastic courses, the *literae inamoenae*, which from his earliest years he abhorred. Zinthius (or Synthius), who was one of the Brethren, and Hegius 'brought a breath of something better', he tells us: but both of them taught only in the higher forms, and Hegius he only heard during his last year, on the festivals when the head master lectured to the whole school together.

A few years later the school numbered 2200 boys. It is difficult to us to imagine such a throng gathered round one man. There were only eight forms, which must therefore have had on an average 275 in each; and even if subdivided into parallel classes, they must still have been uncomfortably large to our modern ideas. On the title-pages of early school-books are sometimes found woodcuts which represent the children sitting, like the Indian schoolboy to-day, in crowds about their master, taking only the barest amount of space, and content with the steps of his desk or even the floor. Some idea of the character of the teaching may be derived from the experiences of Thomas Platter (1499–1582) at Breslau about thirty years later. 'In the school at St. Elizabeth', he says, 'nine B.A.'s read lectures at the same hour and in the same room. Greek had not yet penetrated into that part of the world. No one had any printed books except the praeceptor, who had a Terence.[1] What was read had first to be dictated, then pointed, then construed, and at last explained.'[2] It was a wearisome business for all concerned. The reading of a few lines of text, the punctuation, the elaborate

[1] It is worth remarking that in the fifteenth century Terence was regarded as a prose author, no attempt having been made to determine his metres. As late as 1516 an edition was printed in Paris in prose.

[2] Here, and later on, I follow Mrs. Finn's translation, 1839.

glosses full of wellnigh incomprehensible abbreviations; all dictated slowly enough for a class of a hundred or more to take down every word. Lessons in those days were indeed readings. For a clever boy who was capable of going forward quickly, they must have been great waste of time.

At Deventer Erasmus began with elementary accidence. The books which he first mentions, *Pater meus*, a series of declensions, and *Tempora*, the tenses, that is the conjugations of the verb, were probably local productions of a simple nature which never found their way into print. From this he proceeded to the versified Latin grammars which mediaeval authorities on education had invented to supersede the prose of Priscian and Donatus; metre being more adapted to the learning by heart then so much in fashion. 'Praelegebatur Ebrardus et Joannes de Garlandia', he says: a line or two was read out by the master and then the commentary was dictated—the boys writing down as much as they could catch. Let us see the kind of thing. Here are some extracts from the *Textus Equiuocorum* of John Garland, an Englishman who taught at Toulouse in the thirteenth century.

Latrat et amittit, humilis, vilis, negat, heret:
Est celeste Canis sidus, in amne natat.

'Firstly it is a thing that barks': three verses of quotation follow.

'Secondly it loses; canis being the name for the worst throw with the dice': one verse of quotation.

'Thirdly it is something humble: David to Saul, "After whom is the King of Israel come out? after a dead dog? after a flea?"

Fourthly it is something contemptible: Goliath to David, "Am I a dog that thou comest to me with staves?"

Fifthly it denies, like an apostate: "A dog returned to its vomit."

Sixthly it adheres.' But here the interpreter goes astray under the preoccupation of the times: 'heret significat hereticum et infidelem; hence "It is not good to take the children's bread and cast it unto dogs, that is to heretics and infidels."

Seventhly it is a star; hence are named the dog days, in which that star has dominion.

Eighthly it swims in the sea; the dog fish.'

The qualities of the dog are also expressed in this verse: 'Latrat in ede canis, nat in equore, fulget in astris. Et venit canis originaliter a cano—is.' So Garland, or his commentator, abridged.

Of sal he says:

> Est sal prelatus, equor, sapientia, mimus,
> Sal pultes condit, sal est cibus et reprehendit.

Here again there is a full commentary; but the only interpretation that we need notice is the first, 'Salt denotes a prelate of the Church; for it is said in the Gospels, Ye are the salt of the earth.' When he composed these lines, Garland must surely have had his eye on ecclesiastical preferment.

Another line is interesting, as illustrating the

confusion between c and t in mediaeval manuscripts :

Est katonque malum, katademon nascitur inde.

The commentary runs : 'Kathon est idem quod malum. Inde dicitur kathodemon, i. e. spiritus malignus seu dyabolus, et venit a kathon, i. e. malum, et demon, sciens, quasi mala sciens.' You will notice also the inconstancy of h, and the indifference to orthography which allows the same word to appear as katademon in the text and kathodemon in the commentary.

Garland's *Textus* is mostly Latin ; but in the last composition of his life, the forty-two distiches entitled *Cornutus*, 'one on the horns of a dilemma', he is mainly occupied with Greek words adopted into Latin : using of course Latin characters. Some specimens will show the mediaeval standards of Greek : I quote from the text and commentary edited in 1481 by John Drolshagen, who was master of the sixth class at Zwolle.

Kyria chere geram cuius phīlantrŏpos est bar,
Per te doxa theos nectēn ĕt v̆rānĭcĭs ymas.

In the commentary we are told that Kyria means the Virgin : but we are to be careful not to write it with two r's, for kirrios means a pig (I suppose χοῖρος), and it would never do to say Kirrieleyson. Chere is of course χαῖρε, salue. Geran (geram in the text) is interpreted sanctus, and seems from a lengthy discussion of it to be connected with γέρων and ἱερός.[1] Philantropos (notice the quantities) is Christ, the Saviour. 'Bar Grece est filius Latine.' 'Necten in Greco est venire Latine: vnde dicit Pristianus in primo minoris, antropos necten, i. e. homo venit.' (For this remarkable form I can only suggest ἠνθεῖν or ἥκειν: -en is probably the infinitive; ne might arise from en; and ct, through tt, from th.) Ymas is explained as nobis, not vobis. The construction of the distich is then given: 'Hail, sacred queen, whose son is the lover of men; through thee divine and heavenly glory comes to us.'

Again:

'Clauiculis firmis theos antropos impos et ir mis
Figor ob infirmi cosmos delicta, patir mi.'

Impos = in pedibus. Ir = a hand (probably χείρ, transliterated into hir, and h dropped) and mis is explained as = mei, according to the form which occurs in Plautus and early Latin. The lines are an address from Christ to God, and are interpreted: 'O my father, I God and man am fastened with hard nails in my feet and hands (upon the cross) for the sins of a weak world.'

Another work dictated to Erasmus at Deventer was the metrical grammar of Eberhard of Bethune in Artois, composed in the twelfth century. Its name, *Graecismus*, was based upon a chapter, the eighth, devoted to the elementary study of Greek—a feature which constituted an advance on the

[1] Cf. Gerasmus and Hierasmus as variations of the name Herasmus or Erasmus.

current grammars of the age. A few extracts will show the character of the assistance it offered to the would-be Greek scholar.

> Quod sententia sit bŏlĕ comprobat amphibolīa,
> Quodque fides brŏgĕ sit comprobat Allobroga.

The gloss explains the second line thus: 'Dicitur ab alleos quod est alienum, et broge quod est fides, quasi alienus a fide'; and thus we learn that the Allobroges were a Burgundian people who were always breaking faith with the Romans.

> Constat apud Grecos quod tertia littera cima est,
> Est quoque dulce cĭmēn, inde cĭmētĕrium;
> Est v̆nĭuersalē cătă, fitque cătholicus inde, . . .
> Cāta breuis pariter, cātalogus venit hinc.
> Dic decas esse decem, designans inde decanum . . .
> Delon obscurum, Delius inde venit.
> Ductio sit gogos, hinc isagoga venit.
> Estque geneth mulier, inde genēthēūm.

Here the confusion of c with t begins the misleading; which is carried further by the gloss, 'Genetheum: locus subterraneus vbi habitant mulieres ad laborandum, et dicitur a geneth quod est mulier, et thesis positio, quia ibi ponebantur mulieres ad laborandum'; or 'Genetheum: absconsio subterranea mulierum'.

Estque decem gintos, dicas hinc esse viginti,
Vt pentecoste, coste valebit idem.

Pos quoque pes tibi sit, compos tibi comprobat illud,
Atque pĕdos puer est, hinc pedagogus erit.

Dic zoen animam, dic indē zōĕcăisychen.

This last word appears in eleven different forms in the manuscripts. The gloss interprets it plainly as 'vita mea et anima mea'; but without this aid it must have been unintelligible to most readers, especially in such forms as zoychaysichen, zoycazyche, zoichasichen, zoyasichem.

The 'breath of something better' which Hegius and Zinthius brought was seen in the substitution of the *Doctrinale* of Alexander of Ville-Dieu, near Avranches (*fl.* 1200), as the school Latin grammar. This also is a metrical composition; and it has the merit of being both shorter and also more correct. It was first printed at Venice by Wendelin of Spires (*c.* 1470), and after a moderate success in Italy, twenty-three editions in fourteen years, it was taken up in the North and quickly attained great popularity. By 1500 more than 160 editions had been printed, of the whole or of various parts, and in the next twenty years there were nearly another hundred, before it was superseded by more modern compositions, such as Linacre's grammar, which held the field throughout Europe for a great part of the sixteenth century. The number of Deventer editions of the *Doctrinale* is considerable, mostly containing the glosses of Hegius and Zinthius, which overwhelm the text with commentary; a single distich often receiving two pages of notes, so full of typographical abbreviations and so closely packed together as to be almost illegible. This very fullness, however, probably indicates a change in the method of teaching, which by quickening it up must indeed have put new life into it; for it would clearly have been impossible to dictate such lengthy commentaries, or the boys would have made hardly any progress.

Thirty years ago in England a schoolboy of eleven found himself supplied with abridged Latin and Greek dictionaries, out of which to build up larger familiarity with these languages. Erasmus at Deventer had no such endowments. A school of those days would have been thought excellently equipped if the head master and one or two of his assistants had possessed, in manuscript or in print, one or other of the famous vocabularies in which was amassed the etymological knowledge of the Middle Ages. Great books are costly, and scholars are ever poor. The normal method of acquiring a dictionary was, no doubt, to construct it for oneself; the schoolboy laying foundations and building upon them as he rose from form to form, and the mature student constantly enlarging his plan throughout his life and adding to it the treasures gained by wider reading. A sure method, though necessarily circumscribed, at least in the beginning. We can imagine how men so rooted and grounded must have shaken their heads over 'learning made easy', when the press had begun to diffuse cheap dictionaries, which spared the younger generation such labour.

Though they were scarcely 'for the use of schools', it will repay us to examine some of the mediaeval dictionaries which lasted down to the Renaissance in general use; for they formed the background of educational resources, and from them we can estimate the standards of teaching attained in the late fifteenth century. First the *Catholicon*, compiled by John Balbi, a Dominican of Genoa, and completed on 7 March 1286; a work of such importance to the age we are considering that it was printed at Mainz as early as 1460, and there were many editions later. Badius' at Paris, 1506, for instance, was reprinted in 1510, 1511, 1514. In his preface Balbi announces that his dictionary is to be on the alphabetical principle; and, what is even more surprising to us, he goes on to explain at great length what the alphabetical principle is. Thus: 'I am going to treat of amo and bibo. I shall take amo before bibo, because a is the first letter in amo and b is the first letter in bibo; and a is before b in the alphabet. Again I have to treat of abeo and adeo. I shall take abeo before adeo, because b is the second letter in abeo and d is the second letter in adeo; and b is before d in the alphabet.' And so he goes on: amatus will be treated before amor, imprudens before impudens, iusticia before iustus, polisintheton before polissenus—the two last being from the Greek. 'But note', he continues, 'that in polissenus, s is the fifth letter and also the sixth, because s is repeated there. A repetition is therefore equivalent to a double letter; and thus this arrangement will show when l, m, n, r, s or indeed any other letter is to be doubled. And in order that the reader may find quickly what he seeks, whenever the first or second letter of a word is changed, we shall mark it with azure blue.' His preface ends with an appeal. 'This arrangement I have worked out with great labour; yet not I, but the grace of God with me. I entreat you therefore, reader, do not contemn my work as something rude and barbarous.'

The most striking feature of the dictionary is its etymology. Almost every word is supplied with a derivation, often very far-fetched. Thus glisco is derived from 'glykis, quod est dulcis; que enim dulcia sunt desiderare solemus': gliscere therefore is equivalent to desiderare, crescere, pinguescere and several other words. After this we are not surprised at the following account of a dormouse. 'Glis a glisco: quoddam genus murium quod multum dormit. Et dicitur sic quod sompnus facit glires pingues et crescere.' Here is another piece of natural history. 'Irundo ab aer dicitur: quia non residens sed in aere capiens cibos edat, quasi in aere edens.' There is simplicity in the following: 'Nix a nubes, quia a nube venit.' Again: 'Ouis ab offero vel obluo: quia antiquitus in inicio non tauri sed oues in sacrificio mactarentur. Priscianus vero dicit quod descendit a Greco . . . oys.' Besides his philology the good Dominican was also a theologian; and when he comes to the words upon which his world was built, he cannot dismiss them as lightly as the snow. So Antichristus has two columns, that is to say a folio page: confiteor 1½, conscientia 2¼, ordo 2½, virgo two columns.

Much light is thrown on Balbi's work by the dictionary of his predecessor, Huguitio of Pisa, Bishop of Ferrara († 1210). The title of this, *Liber deriuationum*, indicates its character. Instead of the alphabetical principle the words are arranged according to their etymology; all that are assigned to a given root being grouped together. This made it necessary, or at any rate desirable, to find a derivation for every word; and with ingenuity to aid this was done as far as possible. Besides derivatives even compounds came under the simple root; and in consequence it must have been extremely difficult to find a word unless one already knew a good deal about it. It is no wonder that the book was never printed; although it occurs frequently in the catalogues of mediaeval libraries.

A few examples will suffice. Under capio are found capax, captiuus, capillus, caput with all its derivatives, anceps, praeceps, principium, caper, capus, caupo, cippus, scipio, ⟨s⟩ceptrum; and even cassis and catena. Similarly under nubo come nubes, nebula, nebulo, nix, niger, nimpha, limpha, limpidus. With such a book as one's only support it was clearly of the highest importance to be good at etymology; with ouis, for instance, not to be troubled by Priscian's fanciful derivation from the Greek, but to know that it came from offero, and was therefore to be found under fero; or again to look for hirundo under aer. Nor need we be surprised at the strange derivations upon which arguments were sometimes founded: that Sprenger, the inquisitor, could explain femina 'quia minorem habet et seruat fidem'; or the preacher over whom Erasmus' Folly makes merry, find authority for burning heretics in the Apostle's command 'Haereticum deuita'.

We are now in a position to understand Balbi's performance in the *Catholicon*. From the apologetic tone of his preface it is clear that he felt Huguitio's work to be the really scientific thing, the only book that a scholar would consult: but evidently experience had shown the difficulty of using it, and therefore for the weakness of lesser men like himself he reverted to the sequence of the alphabet. In cumbering himself with derivations, too, he shows that he knows his place. He may have had a glimmering that some of them were absurd; and that Priscian with his reference to the Greek was a safer guide. But to a scholar brought up on Huguitio derivations were of the first importance; and to leave them out would have been only another mark of inferiority.

Beyond Huguitio we may go back to Papias, a learned Lombard (*fl.* 1051), whose Vocabulary was still in use in the fifteenth century, and was printed at Milan in 1476. The editions of it are far fewer than those of the *Catholicon*; a fact which presumably points to the superiority of the later work. Papias also used the alphabetical principle ; and his lengthy explanation of it, which lacks, however, the lucidity of Balbi's, probably implies that his predecessors had adopted the etymological arrangement by derivations, or the divisions of Isidore according to subjects. In a few cases he makes concession to etymology, by giving derivatives under their root, e. g. under ago come all the words derived from it : but he has regard to the weak, and places them also in their right alphabetical position. Not many derivations are given ; but one of them is well known. Lucus is defined as 'locus amenus, vbi multae arbores sunt. Lucus dictus κατὰ ἀντίφρασιν, quia caret luce pro nimia arborum vmbra ; vel a colocando crebris luminibus (*aliter* uiminibus), siue a luce, quod in eo lucebant funalia propter nemorum tenebras.' This in the hands of Balbi becomes 'per contrarium lucus dicitur a lucendo', or, as we say popularly, 'lucus a non lucendo.' December, again, is derived from decem and imbres 'quibus abundare solet' ; and so too the other numbered months.

It is noticeable that Papias has some knowledge of Greek, for derivations in Greek letters occur, e. g. 'Acrocerauni : montes propter altitudinem & fulminum iactus dicti. Graece enim fulmen κεραυνος ceraunos dicitur, et acra ακρα sumitas' ; and a great many Greek and Hebrew words are given transliterated into Latin, ballein, fagein, Ennosigaeus. Like Balbi, Papias travels outside the limits of a mere dictionary, and his interests are not restricted to theology. Aetas draws him into an account of the various ages of the world, regnum into a view of its kingdoms. Carmen provokes 7 columns, $3\frac{1}{2}$ folio pages, on metres ; lapis 2 columns on precious stones. Italy receives 2 columns, and $\frac{3}{4}$ of a column are given to St. Paul. Contrariwise there is often great brevity in his interpretations: 'Samium locus est', 'heroici antiqui', 'mederi curare'. His treatment of miraculum is interesting ; 'A miracle is to raise the dead to life ; but it is a wonder (mirabile) for a fire to be kindled in the water, or for a man to move his ears.' The next heading is mirabilia, for which his examples are taken from the ends of the earth. He begins : 'Listen. Among the Garamantes is a spring so cold by day that you cannot drink it, so hot at night that you cannot put your finger into it.' A fig-tree in Egypt, apples of Sodom, the non-deciduous trees of an island in India—these are the other travellers' tales which serve him for wonders.

The alphabetical method did not hold its own without struggle. It prevailed in Robert Stephanus' Latin *Thesaurus* (1532), the most considerable work of its kind that had been compiled since the invention of printing; but Dolet's Commentaries on the Latin Tongue (1536), are practically a reversion to the arrangement by roots. Henry Stephanus' Greek *Thesaurus* (1572) and Scapula's well-known abridgement of it (1579) are both radical ; and as late as the seventeenth century this method was employed in the first Dictionary of the French Academy, which was designed in 1638 but not published till

1694. That, however, was its last appearance. The preface to the Academy's second Dictionary (1700 and 1718), after comparing the two methods, says: 'The arrangement by roots is the most scientific, and the most instructive to the student; but it is not suited to the impatience of the French people, and so the Academy has felt obliged to abandon it.'[1] The ordinary user of dictionaries to-day would be surprised at being called impatient for expecting the words to be put in alphabetical order.

In mediaeval times there was one very real obstacle to the use of the alphabetical method, and that was the uncertainty of spelling. Both Papias and Balbi allude to it in their prefaces; but it did not deter them from their enterprise. Even in the days of printing language takes a long time to crystallize down into accepted forms, correct and incorrect. You may see Dutchess with a t at Blenheim, well within the eighteenth century, and forgo has only recently decided to give up its e. In the days of manuscripts men spelt pretty much as they pleased, making very free even with their own names; and uncritical copyists, caring only to reproduce the word, and not troubling about the exact orthography of their original, did nothing to check the ever-growing variety. Such licence was agreeable for the imaginative, but it made despairing work for the compilers of dictionaries. Some of their difficulties may be given as examples. In the early days of minuscule writing, when writing-

[1] Cf. R. C. Christie, *Étienne Dolet*, ch. xi.

material was still scarce, to save space it was common to write the letter e with a reversed cedilla beneath it to denote the diphthongs -ae and -oe. In the Middle Ages the cedilla was commonly dropped, leaving the e plain; and so mostly it remained until the sixteenth century revived the diphthong, or at least the two double letters.

At all periods down to 1600, some hands are found in which it is impossible to distinguish between c and t; and hence in mediaeval times, and even later, such forms as fatio, loto, pecieris, licterae are not infrequently found for facio, loco, petieris, litterae. An extreme example of the confusion which this variability must have caused is in the case of the fourteenth-century annalist, Nicholas Trivet, whose surname sometimes appears as Cerseth or Chereth.

The doubling of consonants, too, was often a matter of doubt, and the Middle Ages, possibly again for reasons of space, used many words with single consonants instead of two—difficilimus, Salustius, consumare, comodum, opidum, fuise. The letter h was the source of infinite trouble. Sometimes it was surprisingly omitted, as in actenus, irundo, Oratius, ortus—in the latter cases perhaps under Italian influence; sometimes it appears unexpectedly, as in Therentius, Theutonia, Thurcae, Hysidorus, habundare, and even haspiratio; or in abhominor, where it bolstered up the derivation from homo: or it might change its place from one consonant to another, as in calchographus, cartha.

Papias found it a great trouble, and indeed was quite muddled with it, placing hyppocrita, hippomanes among the h's, but hippopedes and several others under the i's, though without depriving them of initial h. In France, h between two short i's was considered to need support, and so we find michi, nichil, occurring quite regularly. The difficulty of i and y was met by the suppression of the latter; so that though it sometimes appears unexpectedly, as in hystoria, it is only treated as i. Between f and ph there was much uncertainty; phas, phanum, prophanus are well-known forms, or conversely Christofer, flenbothomari, Flegeton. B and p were often confused, as in babtizare, plasphemus; and p made its way into such words as ampnis, dampnum, alumpnus. A triumph of absurd variation is achieved by Alexander Neckam, who begins a sentence 'Coquinarii quocunt'.

With the increased learning of the Renaissance these varieties gradually disappear. The printers, too, rendered good service in promoting uniformity, each firm having its standard orthography for doubtful cases, as printers do to-day. The use of e for ae is abundant in the first books printed North of the Alps; but it steadily diminishes, and by 1500 has almost vanished. In manuscripts, where it was easy to forget to add the cedilla, the plain e lasts much longer. There was also confusion in the reverse direction. Well into the sixteenth century the cedilla is often found wrongly added to words such as puer, equus, eruditus, epistola;

in 1550 the Froben firm was still regularly printing aedo, aeditio; and in the index to an edition of Aquinas, Venice, 1593, aenigma and Aegyptus, spelt in this way, are only to be found under e. Other forms of error persisted long. To the end of his life Erasmus usually wrote irito, oportunus; in 1524 he could still use Oratius. The town of Boppard on the Rhine he styles indifferently Bobardia or Popardia: just as, much later, editors described the elder Camerarius of Bamberg as Bapenbergensis in 1583, as Pabepergensis in 1595. As late as 1540 a little book was printed in Paris to demonstrate that michi and nichil were incorrect.

In such a state of flux we need not wonder that the mediaeval writers of dictionaries found the alphabetical arrangement not the way of simplification they had hoped, but rather to be full of pitfalls; nor again that the men of the Renaissance thought the work of their predecessors so lamentably inadequate. We shall do better to admire in both cases the brilliance and constancy which could achieve so much with such imperfect instruments.

To complete our sketch of the books on which the scholars of the fifteenth century had to rely we may consider two more. The first is the great encyclopaedia of Vincent of Beauvais, a Dominican friar (*c.* 1190–1264). It was printed in 1472–6 by Mentelin at Strasburg, in six enormous volumes; and no one can properly appreciate the magnitude of the work who has not tried to lift these volumes about. Vincent was not the first to attempt this encyclopaedic enterprise, for his work is based on that of another Frenchman, Helinand, who died in 1229. In his preface he states that his prior had urged him to reduce his *Speculum* to a manual; being doubtless an old man, and appalled at these colossal fruits of his friar's industry. But this was too much for the proud author after all his labour. He did, however, consent to cut it up into portions. The *Speculum naturale* gives a description of the world in all its parts, animal and vegetable and mineral; the *Speculum doctrinale* taught how to practise the arts and sciences; the *Speculum historiale* embraced the world's history down to 1250; and the *Speculum morale,* which is perhaps not by Vincent, found room for the philosophies.

But few libraries can have possessed this work in full. Our other book was much more compassable and more widely circulated. Its author was a certain Johannes Marchesinus, of whom so little is known that his date has been put both at 1300 and at 1466. Even the title of the book was uncertain. Marchesinus names it Mammotrectus or Mammetractus, which he explains as 'led by a pedagogue'; but a current form of the name was Mammothreptus, which was interpreted as 'brought up by one's grandmother'. The book consists of a commentary on the whole Bible, chapter by chapter; and also upon the *Legenda Sanctorum,* upon various sermons and homilies, responses, antiphons, and hymns, with notes on the Hebrew months, ecclesiastical vestments, and other subjects likely to be useful to students in the Church, especial emphasis being laid on pronunciation and quantity. It was intended, Marchesinus tells us in his preface, for the use of the poor clergy, to aid them in writing sermons and in reading difficult Hebrew names; and from the sympathy with which he enters into their troubles, it seems clear that he knew them from personal experience.

From its scope the book might be expected to be as large as Vincent's *Speculum*, but in fact it can be printed in a quarto volume. It was not intended to compete with the great commentaries of Peter the Lombard, or Nicholas Lyra, or Hugh of St. Victor, which fill many folios. It was to be within reach of the poor parish priest, and so must not be costly. But the surprising part of the book is its triviality. With so little space available, one would have expected to find nothing admitted that was not important: but the fact is that it has nothing which is not elementary. There is nothing historical, nothing theological, only a few simple points of grammar and quantity. For example, in the story of Deborah, Judges iv, the commentary runs as follows:

2. Sisara: middle syllable short.
4. Debbora: middle syllable short. Prophetes masc., Prophetis fem.; meaning, propheta.
10. Accersitis: last syllable but one long; meaning, vocatis.
15. Perterreo, perterres; meaning, in pauorem conuertere. Active.

17. Cinei (the Kenites): middle syllable long.
15. Desilio, desilis, desilii or desiliui: middle syllable short in trisyllables in the present; meaning, de aliquo salire siue descendere festinanter.
21. clauus, masc., claui: meaning, acutum ferrum.
malleus, masc., mallei: meaning, martellus.
tempus, neut.: meaning, pars capitis, for which some people say timpus.

For Daniel vi, the story of Daniel in the lions' den, the commentary is even briefer:

6. surripuerunt: meaning, falso suggesserunt. Surripio, surripis, surrepsi (!): meaning, latenter rapere, subtrahere, furari.
10. comperisset; meaning, cognouisset. Comperio, comperis, comperi: fourth conjugation.
20. affatus: meaning, allocutus. From affor, affaris; and governs the accusative.

We must not exalt ourselves above the author. He is very humble. 'Let any imperfections in the book', says his preface, 'be attributed to me: and if there is anything good, let it be thought to have come from God.' He gave them of his best, explaining away such as he could of the difficulties which had confronted him. But one can imagine the disgust of even a moderate scholar if, wishing to study the Bible more carefully, he could obtain access to nothing better than Mammotrectus.

Though Erasmus has not much to tell us of his time at Deventer, a fuller account of the school may be found in the autobiography of John Butzbach (*c.* 1478–1526), who for the last nineteen years of his life was Prior of Laach.[1] Indeed, his narrative is so detailed and so illustrative of the age that it may well detain us here. He was the son of a weaver in the town of Miltenberg (hence Piemontanus) on the Maine, above Aschaffenburg. At the age of six he was put to school and already began to learn Latin; one of his nightly exercises that he brought home with him being to get by heart a number of Latin words for vocabulary. After a few years he came into trouble with his master for laziness and truancy, and received a severe beating; his mother intervened and got the master dismissed from his post, and Butzbach was removed from the school.

An opportunity then offered for him to get a wider education. The son of a neighbour who had commenced scholar, returned home for a time, and offered to take Butzbach with him when he went off again to pursue his courses for his degree. The consent of his parents was obtained; and the scholar having received a liberal contribution towards expenses, and Butzbach being equipped with new clothes, the pair set out together. The boy was now ten, and looked forward hopefully to the future; but the scholar quickly showed himself in his true

[1] Butzbach's manuscripts from Laach are now in the University Library at Bonn, but have never been printed. I have used a German translation by D. J. Becker, Regensburg, 1869.

colours. He treated Butzbach as a fag, made him trudge behind carrying the larger share of their bundles, and when they came to an inn feasted royally himself off the money given to him for the boy, leaving him to the charity of the innkeepers. At the end of two months the money was spent, and they had found no place of settlement. Henceforward Butzbach was set to beg, going from house to house in the villages they passed, asking for food; and when this failed to produce enough, he was required to steal. The scholar treated him shamefully and beat him often; and as it was a well-known practice for fags, when begging, to eat up delicacies at once, instead of bringing them in, Butzbach was sometimes subjected to the regular test, being required to fill his mouth with water and then spit it out into a basin for his master to examine whether there were traces of fat.

The scholar's aim was to find some school, having attached to it a Bursa or hostel, in which they could obtain quarters; apparently he was not yet qualified for a university. They made their way to Bamberg, but there was no room for them in the Bursa. So on they went into Bohemia, where at the town of Kaaden the rector of the school was able to allot them a room—just a bare, unfurnished chamber, in which they were permitted to settle. Such teaching as Butzbach received was spasmodic and ineffectual, and after two years of this bondage he ran away. For the next five years he was in Bohemia in private service, longing for home, hating his durance among the heathen, as he called the Bohemians for following John Hus, but lacking courage to make his escape from masters who could send horsemen to scour the countryside for fugitive servants and string them up to trees when caught. However, at length the opportunity came, and after varying fortunes, Butzbach made his way home to Miltenberg, to find his father dead and his mother married again.

For the substantial accuracy of Butzbach's narrative his character is sufficient warranty. He was a pious, honest man, and at the time when he wrote his autobiography at the request of his half-brother Philip, he was already a monk at Laach. But the picture of a young student's sufferings under an elder's cruelty can be paralleled with surprising closeness from the autobiography of Thomas Platter, mentioned above; the wandering from one school to another, the maltreatment, the begging, the enforced stealing, all these are reproduced with just the difference of surroundings.

Platter's account of his life at Breslau is worth quoting. 'I was ill three times in one winter, so that they were obliged to bring me into the hospital; for the travelling scholars had a particular hospital and physicians for themselves. Care was taken of the patients, and they had good beds, only the vermin were so abundant that, like many others, I lay much rather upon the floor than in the beds. Through the winter the fags lay upon the floor in the school, but the Bacchants in small chambers, of which at St. Elizabeth's there were several hundreds.

But in summer, when it was hot, we lay in the churchyard, collected together grass such as is spread in summer on Saturdays in the gentlemen's streets before the doors, and lay in it like pigs in the straw. When it rained, we ran into the school, and when there was thunder, we sang the whole night with the Subcantor, responses and other sacred music. Now and then after supper in summer we went into the beerhouses to beg for beer. The drunken Polish peasants would give us so much that I often could not find my way to the school again, though only a stone's throw from it.' Platter wrote his autobiography at the age of 73, when his memories of his youth must have been growing dim; but though on this account we must not press him in details, his main outlines are doubtless correct.

On his return, Butzbach was apprenticed to Aschaffenburg, to learn the trade of tailoring; and having mastered this, he procured for himself, in 1496, the position of a lay-brother in the Benedictine Abbey of Johannisberg in the Rheingau, opposite Bingen. His duties were manifold. Besides doing the tailoring of the community, he was expected to make himself generally useful: to carry water and fetch supplies, to look after guests, to attend the Abbot when he rode abroad (on one occasion he was thrown thus into the company of Abbot Trithemius of Sponheim, whose work on the Ecclesiastical writers of his time he afterwards attempted to carry on), to help in the hay harvest, and in gathering the grapes. Before a year was out he grew tired of these humble duties, and bethought him anew of his father's wish that he should become a professed monk. He had omens too. One morning his father appeared to him as he was dressing, and smiled upon him. Another day he was sitting at his work and talking about his wish with an old monk who was sick and under his care. On the wall in front of his table he had fastened a piece of bread, to be a reminder of the host and of Christ's sufferings. Suddenly this fell to the ground. The old man started up from his place by the stove, and steadying his tottering limbs cried out aloud that this was a sign that the wish was granted. He had the reputation among his fellows of being a prophet and had foretold the day of his own death. Butzbach accepted the omen, and obtained leave to go to school again.

His choice was Deventer. One of the brethren wrote him an elegant letter to Hegius applying for admission; and though, as he says, he answered no questions in his entrance examination (which appears to have been oral), on the strength of the letter he was admitted and placed in the seventh class, a young man of twenty amongst the little boys who were making a beginning at grammar. But he had no means of support except occasional jobs of tailor's work, and hunger drove him back to Johannisberg. There he might have continued, had not a chance meeting with his mother, when he had ridden over to Frankfort with the Abbot, given him a new spur. She could not bear to think of his remaining a Lollhard, that is a lay-brother, all his days;

and pressing money privily into his hands, she besought the Abbot to let him return to Deventer. In August 1498 he was there again, was examined by Hegius, and was placed this time in the lowest class, the eighth, in company with a number of stolid louts, who had fled to school to escape being forced to serve as soldiers. There was reason in their fears. The Duke of Gueldres was at war with the Bishop of Utrecht. A hundred prisoners had been executed in the three days before Butzbach's return, and as he strode into Deventer to take up his books again, he may have seen their scarce-cold bodies swinging on gibbets against the summer sunset. The schoolboy of to-day works in happier surroundings.

Butzbach's career henceforward was fortunate. He was taken up by a good and pious woman, Gutta Kortenhorff, who without regular vows had devoted herself to a life of abstinence and self-sacrifice; taking special pleasure in helping young men who were preparing for the Franciscan or the reformed Benedictine Orders. For nine months Butzbach lived in her house, doubtless out of gratitude rendering such service as he could to his kind patroness. From the eighth class he passed direct into the sixth, and at Easter 1499 he was promoted into the fifth. This entitled him to admission to the Domus Pauperum maintained by the Brethren of the Common Life for boys who were intending to become monks; and so he transferred himself thither for the remainder of his course. But he suffered much from illness, and five several times made up his mind to give up and return home—once indeed this was only averted by a swelling of his feet, which for a prolonged period made it impossible for him to walk. After six months in the fifth, and a year in the fourth class, he was moved up into the third, thus traversing in little over two years what had occupied Erasmus for something like nine.

Butzbach was by temperament inclined to glorify the past; in the present he himself had a share, and therefore in his humility he thought little of it. In consequence we must not take him too literally in his account of the condition of the school; but it is too interesting to pass over. 'In the old days', he says, 'Deventer was a nursery for the Reformed Orders; they drew better boys, more suited to religion, out of the fifth class, than they do now out of the second or first, although now much better authors are read there. Formerly there was nothing but the Parables of Alan ⟨of Lille, *fl.* 1200⟩, the moral distichs of Cato, Aesop's Fables, and a few others, whom the moderns despise; but the boys worked hard, and made their own way over difficulties. Now when even in small schools the choicest authors are read, ancient and modern, prose and poetry, there is not the same profit; for virtue and industry are declining. With the decay of that school, religion also is decaying, especially in our Order, which drew so many good men from there. And yet it is not a hundred years since our reformation.'

He does not indicate how far back he was turning

his regretful gaze; whether to the early years of the fifteenth century when Nicholas of Cues was a scholar at Deventer, or to the more recent times of Erasmus, who was about three school-generations ahead of him. But of the books used there in the last quarter of the fifteenth century we can form a clear notion from the productions of the Deventer printers, Richard Paffraet and Jacobus of Breda. School-books then as now were profitable undertakings, if printed cheap enough for the needy student; and Paffraet, with Hegius living in his house, must have had plenty of opportunities for anticipating the school's requirements. Between 1477 and 1499 he printed Virgil's Eclogues, Cicero's *De Senectute* and *De Amicitia*, Horace's *Ars Poetica*, the *Axiochus* in Agricola's translation, Cyprian's Epistles, Prudentius' poems, Juvencus' *Historia Euangelica*, and the *Legenda Aurea* : also the grammar of Alexander with the commentary of Synthius and Hegius, Agostino Dato's *Ars scribendi epistolas*, Aesop's Fables, and the *Dialogus Creaturarum*, the latter two being moralized in a way which must surely have pleased Butzbach. Jacobus of Breda, who began printing at Deventer in 1486, produced Virgil's Eclogues, Cicero's *De Senectute* and *De Officiis*, Boethius' *De consolatione philosophiae* and *De disciplina scholarium*, Aesop, a poem by Baptista Mantuanus, the 'Christian Virgil', Alan of Lille's *Parabolae*, Alexander, two grammatical treatises by Synthius and the *Epistola mythologica* of Bartholomew of Cologne.

This last, as being the work of a master in the school, deserves attention ; and also for its intrinsic interest. As its title implies, it is cast in the form of a letter, addressed to a friend Pancratius ; and it is dated from Deventer 10 July 1489—nine years before Butzbach entered the school. It opens with the customary apologies, and after some ordinary topics the writer, Bartholomew, says that he is sending back some books borrowed from Pancratius, including a Sidonius which he has had on loan for three years. At this point there is a transformation. Sidonius is personified and becomes the centre of a series of semi-comic incidents, which afford an opportunity for introducing various words for the common objects of everyday life ; and a glossary explains many of these with precision. There is a long and vivid account of the waking of Sidonius from his three years' slumber. The door has to be broken open, and Sidonius is found lying to all appearances dead. A feather burnt under his nose produces slight signs of life ; and when a good beating with the bar of the door is threatened, he at length rouses himself. Servants come in, and their different duties are described. They fall to quarrelling and become uproarious ; and in the scuffle Sidonius is hurt. A lotion is prepared for his bruises, and he is offered diet suitable for an invalid : boiled sturgeon, washed down with wine or beer, the latter being from Bremen or Hamburg.

Afterwards the room is cleared up, and thus an opportunity is given to describe it. Then a table is spread for the rest of the party, and the various requisites are specified—tablecloth and napkins, pewter plates, earthenware mugs, a salt-cellar and two brass stands for the dishes. Bread is put round to each place, chairs are brought up with cushions; and jugs of wine and beer placed in the centre of the table. Finally a basin is brought with ewer and towel for the guests to wash their hands, and as one o'clock strikes, dinner appears, and all sit down together, including the servants. After the meal a dice-box and board are produced; but one of the guests demurs, and it is put aside. In the conversation that ensues it is arranged that Sidonius shall go back to his master next morning after breakfast. The servant who is to accompany him asks that they may go in a carriage; but this is overruled, because of a recent accident in which one had been upset, and it is determined that a Spanish palfrey of easy paces shall be provided for Sidonius. At six supper is served; and then the curtain falls, the letter relapsing into normal matters—inquiries for a Euclid, regrets at being unable to send to Pancratius Hyginus and the *Astronomica* of Manilius.

It is clear that the object of the book, which is of no great length, was to give boys correct Latin words for the material objects of their daily life: something like Bekker's *Gallus* and *Charicles* on a small scale. In carrying out this idea Bartholomew of Cologne has provided us with a sketch of the world that he knew.

III

MONASTERIES

Erasmus was not fitted for the monastic life. This is not to say that he was a bad man. Few men outside the ranks of the holy have worked harder or made greater sacrifices to do God service. But his was a free spirit. His work could only be done in his own way; and to live according to another's rule fretted him beyond endurance. His experience in the matter was not fortunate. In 1483 his mother died of plague at Deventer, whither she had accompanied him. His father recalled him next year to Gouda, but died soon afterwards; and his guardians then sent him with his elder brother to a school kept by the Brethren of the Common Life at Hertogenbosch—doubtless to a Domus Pauperum for intending monks, such as Butzbach entered at Deventer; for in this connexion Erasmus describes the schools of the Brethren as seminaries for the regular orders. After two years they returned to Gouda, and Erasmus begged to be sent to a university; but no means were forthcoming, and the guardian prevailed upon the elder brother Peter to enter the monastery of Sion, near Delft. Erasmus held out for some time; but he was without resources and the influences at work upon him were strong. One day he fell in with a school-friend, Cornelius of Woerden, who had recently entered the house of Augustinian canons at Steyn, near Gouda. In his loneliness any friend was welcome. He paid visits to Steyn and saw that the life there offered leisure and even possibilities of study; Cornelius, too, seemed inclined to be a ready companion in literary pursuits. Urged by his guardian, invited by his friend, he gave way at length to the double pressure and entered Steyn.

After a novitiate of a year, during which life was made easy to him, he took his canonical vows; and soon began to repent of the step he had made. For about seven years he lived in what seemed to him a prison. There were, no doubt, good men amongst his fellow-canons. In all his diatribes against monasticism he was ready to admit that the Orders contained plenty of God-fearing souls, doing their duty honestly; and the evidence shows clearly enough that this was correct. It is, however, equally true that there were mediocrities among them, and even worse; men with low standards and no ideals, who brought their fellows to shame. Vows in those days were indissoluble, except in rare cases; as a rule it was only by flight and disappearance for ever that a man could escape social disgrace and the penalties threatened by the spiritual arm to a renegade monk. To-day, when orders can be laid down at the holder's will, the Church of England contains priests of whom it cannot get rid.

The good, even when they rule, do not always lead; nor are they always learned. Erasmus found the atmosphere of Steyn hopelessly distasteful. It was not that he was prevented from study. His compositions of this period show a wide acquaintance with the classics and the Fathers; and his style, though it had not yet attained to the ease and lucidity of his later years, has much of the elegance beyond which his contemporaries never advanced. The fact, too, that he left Steyn to become Latin Secretary to a powerful bishop implies that he must have had many opportunities for study and have made good use of them. But from what he says it is clear that the tone of the place was set by the mediocrities. We need not suppose that vice was rampant among them, to shock the young and enthusiastic scholar. There was quite enough to daunt him in the prospect of a life spent among the narrow-minded. Sinners who feel waves of repentance may be better house-mates than those who have worldly credit enough to make them self-satisfied.

Fortunately all houses of religion were not alike, any more than colleges are alike to-day. Butzbach's lot was very different; and it is a pleasant contrast to turn to his experiences at Laach, an important Benedictine abbey some miles west of Andernach. In the autumn of 1500, when he had been two years at Deventer, there appeared one day in the school the Steward of the Abbey of Niederwerth, an island in the Rhine below Coblenz. What the business was which had brought him from his own monastery, is not stated; but he had also been asked to do some recruiting for the Benedictines at Laach. The Abbot there was nephew of the Prior at Niederwerth, and had taken this opportunity to extend his quest further afield. The Steward brought with him letters from the Abbot to the Rector of Deventer, now Ostendorp, and also to the Brethren of the Common Life, asking for some good and well-educated young men. The Rector's first appeal evoked no response; so the Steward went on about his business. After three weeks he returned, having visited other schools, but bringing no one with him. Once more Ostendorp addressed the third and fourth classes in impressive words. But all seemed in vain. The students had paid their school fees for the half-year, and were ashamed to ask for them back from the Rector and other teachers—into whose pockets they appear to have gone direct. Their money paid for board and lodging would have been sacrificed also. It happened, too, to be exceptionally cold—not the weather in which any one would lightly set out on a journey. We must remember that the calendar had not yet been rectified, and that they were about ten days nearer to midwinter than their dates show.

On occasions the whole school came together to hear the Rector—it was at such times, Erasmus tells us, that he heard Hegius. At one of these gatherings during the Steward's second visit Butzbach was sitting next to two friends from his own part of the world, Peter of Spires and Paul of Kitzingen. They were above him in the school, having passed their entrance examination before the Rector with such credit that they were placed at once in the third class—a rare distinction—and Paul indeed at the end of his first half-year had come out top and passed into the second. The friends talked together of the life of the cloister, of the happiness of study amid the practice of holiness and in the presence of God. At the end Peter and Butzbach sought out the Steward and gave him their names: Paul, the brilliant leader of the trio, remained behind in the world, and became a professor at Cologne.

Butzbach said farewell to the masters who had taught him, and to his various benefactors in the town, all of whom applauded his decision. On St. Barbara's Day, 4 Dec. 1500, the party set out, and were accompanied out of the town by students who swarmed about them like bees; Butzbach, when they at length took leave, urging them to follow his example. Two days later they were at Emmerich, and after crossing the Rhine on the ice, so bitter was the frost, they were overtaken by the night at a convent and sought shelter. It proved to be a house of Brigittines, with separate orders of men and women. One of the party, a priest from Deventer, had a kinswoman among the nuns, but was not allowed to see her. On 8 December the feast of the Conception of the Virgin, as they passed through a village, the two priests asked leave to say a mass for themselves in the parish church; and only with difficulty obtained it from the pfarrer in charge, so great was the jealousy between seculars and regulars. At night they found hospitality in a Benedictine house at Neuss, where Butzbach notes the peculiarity—which he discusses at length but is quite unable to explain—that no one could be accepted as a monk with the name of Peter.

Next day the party was obliged to divide. Peter of Spires, who from the first had been ailing and easily tired, was suffering acute pain from a sore on his finger; so Butzbach remained behind with him in a village, while the others went on to Cologne. After twenty-four hours the sufferer was no better; and as sleep for either of them seemed impossible, they arose at midnight, hired a cart, and journeying under the stars, arrived at Cologne just as the gates were being opened. They rejoined their friends, and the whole party was entertained in the house of a rich widow, whose son, recently dead, had been a monk at Niederwerth.

The Steward had business at Cologne; so for two days the young men were free to wander about the town, looking into the churches and worried by the schoolboy tricks of the university students. Three days journeying brought them late at night and dead tired to Niederwerth. The aged Prior—he had been sixty years in the monastery—on learning their destination showed them great courtesy and kindness; and when they had supped, insisted, despite all their protests, on washing their feet himself. Next day he showed them over the monastery, took them into the rooms where the brethren were at work, and explained what each of them had to do: 'just as though we were his equals,' says Butzbach, on whom his modesty and friendliness made a deep impression. Indeed, his conversation greatly strengthened them in their determination to enter the religious life; although he did not conceal from them the temptations which they might expect, from the Devil.

On 17 December he gave them leave to proceed, and sent one of the monastery servants and a lay-brother to escort them. Their way lay through Coblenz; and Peter as a weaker vessel was sent on, to go slowly ahead with the lay-brother, whilst the servant and Butzbach stopped in the town to execute some commissions. But they had under-estimated Peter's weakness. After a midday meal the second pair set out briskly, in the comfortable reflection that the others were already part-way to Laach. To their disgust as they crossed the bridge over the Moselle, they found Peter and his companion lolling outside an inn, unable to talk properly or to stand upright. The Prior's warning against the Devil had been speedily justified. Peter had been tempted to spend his last day of freedom in a carouse, and every penny he possessed had gone over a fine dinner and costly wines.

To Butzbach this was the more serious, because he had given his purse to Peter to carry, and all that had gone too. Johannisberg still had strong ties for him. He had found peace there and made friends, and it was near his home. Many times, at silent moments as he journeyed along from Deventer, it had come into his head to wonder whether Laach too could give him peace, whether he could settle so far off. Now, if the old ties should be too strong to resist, thanks to Peter, he would have to set out on his way penniless.

Sharp words brought the offenders to some measure of their senses; but it was a dismal party that splashed along the muddy roads that December afternoon. Evening brought them to Saffig, and hospitable reception in the house of George von Leyen, brother of the Prior of Niederwerth and father of the Abbot to whom they were going; and the parents' praises of their son's goodness and kindness were comforting to hear. Ten miles next morning brought them to Laach; and when they came over the hill, and saw the great abbey with its towers and dome beside the lake, which even in winter could smile amid its woods, Butzbach felt that in all his travels he had seen no sight more lovely. Their guide led them straight into the church, and as Butzbach's eye glanced along the plain Romanesque columns, past the gorgeous tomb of the founder, to the dim splendours of the choir, the words of the familiar Psalm rose to his lips: 'Haec requies mea in saeculum saeculi; hic habitabo, quoniam elegi eam.' Peace had come to him at once, and he received it.

After a generous meal in the refectory they were brought in to the tall, dignified Abbot; and while they stood before him answering his questions, they felt that he had not been praised more highly than was his due. Abbot and Prior took them round the monastery; the latter a busy little man in whom they could hardly recognize so exalted a dignitary.

At the back they found the brethren busy with the week's washing. All crowded round them, full of questions and congratulations and pleasant laughter. For three days they were lodged in the guest-chambers, and then the Prior asked them whether they stood firm in their wish to enter the Order. On their assent he expounded to them the severities of the life, the self-abnegation that would be required of them, bidding them consider whether they could face it; at the same time instructing them in all the customs and practices of the house. The dress was put upon them, they were led into the convent and cells allotted to them; and told that till St. Benedict's Day (21 March) they would be on probation. Before the day came Peter's spirit faltered, and he went. But his weakness was not for long. He repented and found his peace in a Cistercian house near Worms; and Butzbach's sympathy went with him, back to the Upper Germany which both loved.

The time of probation was hard to Butzbach; not because of the life, which the good Prior tempered to his tenderness, but through the temptations of the Devil, who seemed ever present with him. He was specially tormented with the thought of Johannisberg, and the feeling that he had deserted it. But the wise heads in charge of him gave comfort and stablishment; and he persevered. On the Founder's Day, 1501, he entered upon the novitiate, which was followed a year later by his profession; and in 1503 he was sent to Trèves and ordained priest.

In the course of his numerous writings Butzbach

gives sketches of many of the inmates of Laach. The senior brother at the time of his arrival was Jacob of Breden in Westphalia, a man of strong character and force of will. As a boy, when at school at Cleves, he was laughed at for his provincial accent; and therefore determined henceforward to speak nothing but Latin, with the result that he acquired a complete mastery of it. He had at first joined the Brethren of the Common Life at Zwolle, then became a Benedictine in St. Martin's at Cologne, and came to Laach to introduce the Bursfeld reforms. So tender-hearted was he that he would not kill even the insects which worried him, but would catch them and throw them out of window. John of Andernach is mentioned as having appeared to the brethren after his death; and he and Godfrey of Cologne are praised for their skill in astronomy. We hear of various activities among the monks. One is good at writing, another at dictating and correcting, another has taste in painting flowers and illuminating. Henry of Coblenz combined the offices of precentor, master of the robes, gardener, glazier and barber; and also unofficial counsellor to the young, who frequently turned to him for sympathy. Antony of St. Hubert, besides the care of the refectory, was bee-master and hive-maker; and a great preacher in German, though he had come to Laach knowing only his native French. At the end of the list came the lay-brothers and the pensioners (donati), one of whom was nearly 100.

Shortly after his ordination Butzbach was

appointed master of the novices, to superintend their education—which included learning the Psalter by heart—until the time of their profession. He protested his unfitness, but the Abbot held him to it nevertheless. The standard of his pupils was low: many of them, though they came as Bachelors and Masters of Arts from the universities, he judged not so good as boys in the sixth form at Deventer. But he found lecturing in Latin difficult; and so to make up his deficiencies he set himself to read all the Latin classics and Fathers that he could find. One day two young kinsmen of the Abbot were at dinner. They had been at Deventer and then at Paris, and were full of their studies. Butzbach as novice-master represented the humanities, and was called upon for a poem. Readiness was not his strong point; as a preacher he never could overcome his nervousness. He asked leave to retire to his cell, and there in solitude wrung out some verses of compliment; which found such favour that, to his regret, he was often called upon again.

In 1507, when only thirty, he was made Prior, and thus became responsible for much of the management of the abbey. In spite of this he kept up his studies; but only at the cost of great physical efforts, robbing himself of sleep and working through long hours of the night. To this period, 1507–9, belongs his most considerable undertaking, an *Auctarium de scriptoribus ecclesiasticis*, which had its origin in his admiration for Trithemius. In his Johannisberg days, as we have seen, he had met the great historian-abbot, though in a humble capacity. His own Abbot shared with Trithemius the duty of making the triennial visitations of the Benedictine houses in that district; and Butzbach, as the Abbot's servant, often rode with them. Trithemius noticed the young lay-brother who seemed so interested in study, and occasionally gave him a word of encouragement. Indeed it was the story of Trithemius' life—repeated with wonder by many lips—which had spurred Butzbach on to go to Deventer: how as a boy he had worked with his stepfather in the mill at Trittenheim, and at twenty-one was still labouring with his hands. One day he was carting material for a new pilgrimage-church on the hill, when the call came to him. He returned home, put up his horse and wagon, and without a word to any one walked off to Niederwesel to begin learning grammar amongst the little boys; and yet in a short time he had risen to be Abbot, and had won a wide reputation.

At Laach Butzbach for the first time set eyes on Trithemius' works. One of these was a *Liber de scriptoribus ecclesiasticis*, printed by John Amorbach at Basle in 1494—a sort of theological *Who's Who*, giving the names of authors ancient and modern with lists of their writings. Butzbach continued it with an *Auctarium*, into which he hooked almost every writer he could find, whether ecclesiastical or not. It is a large book, still remaining in manuscript at Bonn, as it was written out for him by two very inefficient novices. The date of its composition is abundantly indicated by the notes with which he terminates his notices of living authors: 'Viuit adhuc anno quo hec scribimus 158' or 159.[1] Such a compilation, in so far as it deals with contemporary writers, might have had considerable value; but unfortunately, like some of Trithemius' work, it is an uncritical performance and contains ridiculous blunders, which impair the credit of its statements when they cannot be checked. Industry and devotion to learning are not the sole qualifications for a scholar.

But it was not altogether a happy time for Butzbach, even though he was honoured by correspondence with Trithemius. There were few among the monks who actually sympathized with his studies; and from a certain section they brought him actual persecution. When, as Prior, he emphasized before the brethren the section in Benedict's rule which enjoins to study, they mocked at him. 'No learning, no doubts' said one. 'Much learning doth make thee mad' said another. 'Knowledge puffeth up' said a third; and heeded not his gentle reply, 'but love edifieth'. They protested against his allowing the novices to read Latin poetry. They appealed to the Visitor and got the supplies of money for the library cut off; even what he earned himself by saying masses for the dead was no longer allowed to be appropriated to him for the purchase of books. Finally when the visitation came round in 1509, they delated him for spending too much time on

[1] = 1509. By a reverse process Bruno Amorbach writes 10507 for 1507.

writing, to the neglect of the business of the monastery. But here they overreached themselves. The Visitors called for his books, opened them and saw that they were good—possibly they found their own names among the ecclesiastical writers. The Prior was acquitted, and the mouths of his enemies were stopped.

One cause of dissension in monasteries at this period was the existence of an unreformed element among the monks; though in Butzbach's time it had probably disappeared at Laach. Ever since the Oriental practice of monasticism spread into the West, Christendom has seen a continual series of endeavours towards better and purer ideals of human life. Of all the monastic orders the Benedictine (520) was the oldest and the most widely spread. But time had relaxed the strictness of its observance; and indeed some of the younger orders, such as the Cluniac (910) and the Cistercian (1098), had their origins in efforts after a more godly life than what was then offered under the Benedictine rule, the strictness of which they sought to restore. In the fifteenth century reform of the monasteries was once more in the air.[1] In 1422 a chapter of the Benedictine houses in the provinces of Trèves and Cologne met at Trèves to discuss the question, which had been raised again at the Council of Constance, and to consider various schemes. The

[1] At this point and again later about Chezal-Benoît I have made much use of Dom Berlière's *Mélanges d'histoire bénédictine*, 3e série, 1901.

Abbot of St. Matthias' at Trèves, John Rode, learning of the stricter code practised in St. James' at Liège since the thirteenth century, introduced it into his house; borrowing four monks from St. James' to help him in the process. A few years later John Dederoth of Minden, Abbot of Bursfeld near Göttingen, after examining the new practice at Trèves, decided to follow Rode's example, and carried off four brethren from St. Matthias' to Bursfeld. His influence led a number of neighbouring Benedictine houses to adopt the new rule; and very soon a Bursfeld Union or Congregation was formed of monasteries which had embraced what Butzbach calls 'our reformation', with annual chapters and triennial visitations.

By the end of the fifteenth century there were more than a hundred constituents of the Congregation. The usual method of introducing the new practice was, as Rode and Dederoth had done, to borrow a number of monks from a house already reformed, who either settled in the new house or returned home when their work was done. As may be supposed, the reforms were not everywhere welcomed. A zealous Abbot or Prior returning with his band of foreigners was often met by opposition and even forcible resistance. When Jacob of Breden, Butzbach's 'senior brother', came in 1471 with seven others from St. Martin's at Cologne to renew a right spirit in Laach, a number of the older monks resented it, especially when he was made Prior for the purpose. One cannot but sympathize with them. Jacob was only thirty-two, and it is a delicate matter setting one's elders in the right way. At length the seniors became exasperated and took to violence. Not content with belabouring him in his cell, they attacked him one night with swords, and he only escaped by leaping out of the dormitory window. The rest of his company were ejected, and for three years found shelter in St. Matthias' at Trèves, the parent house of the new rule; and it was not till 1474 that the Archbishop, with the Pope's permission and the co-operation of the civil official of the district, forced his way into Laach and turned out the recalcitrants.

But this movement for reform was not confined to Germany nor to the Benedictines. In the beginning of the fifteenth century the house of Augustinian canons at Windesheim near Zwolle instituted for itself a new and stricter set of statutes, and soon gathered round it nearly a hundred houses of both sexes, forming the Windesheim Congregation: besides which, other monasteries bound themselves into smaller bodies to observe the new statutes. Thus, for instance, Erasmus' convent at Steyn was a member of the Chapter of Sion, with only a few others; two of which were St. Mary's at Sion, near Delft, to which his brother Peter belonged, and St. Michael's at Hem, near Schoonhoven. The fame of Windesheim spread into France. In two successive years—1496, 7—parties were invited thence to reform French Benedictine houses. The first, headed by John Mauburn of Brussels, was brought in by the Abbot of St. Severinus' at Château-Landon near Fontainebleau.

It was completely successful and Château-Landon was made the head of a new Chapter: after which Mauburn proceeded to reform the Abbey of Livry, a few miles to the north-east of Paris. The second mission, though promoted by influential men in Paris, had less result. St. Victor's, the Benedictine Abbey which the Bishop of Paris wished to reform, was one of the most important in his diocese; and its inmates were averse from the proposed changes. For nine months the mission from Windesheim sat in Paris, expounding, demonstrating, hoping to persuade. One of the party, Cornelius Gerard of Gouda, an intimate friend of Erasmus' youth, enjoyed himself greatly among the manuscripts in the abbey library; but that was all. In August 1498 they went home, leaving St. Victor's as they had found it.

The strenuous endeavours made at this time towards monastic reform from within may be illustrated from the lives of Guy Jouveneaux (Juuenalis) and the brothers Fernand. Jouveneaux was a scholar of eminence and professor in the University of Paris. Charles Fernand was a native of Bruges, who, in spite of defective eyesight, which made it necessary for him regularly to employ a reader, had studied in Italy, had been Rector of Paris University, 1485–6, and had attained to considerable skill in both classical learning and music. John Fernand, the younger brother, also excelled in both these branches of study. Symphorien Champier, the Lyons physician, speaks of him with Jouveneaux as his teacher in

Paris. Charles VIII made him chief musician of the royal chapel.

In 1479 Peter du Mas became Abbot of the Benedictine house at Chezal Benoît, which lay in the forests, ten miles to the South of Bourges. His first care was to restore the buildings, which had been partially destroyed during the English wars earlier in the century. When that was achieved, he set himself to reform the conditions of religious observance, and for that purpose invited a band of monks from Cluny. His policy was continued by his successor, Martin Fumeus, 1492–1500, and a bull was obtained from Alexander VI in 1494 permitting the foundation of a Congregatio Casalina, which was joined by a large number of Benedictine houses in the neighbourhood: St. Sulpice, St. Laurence and St. Menulphus at Bourges, St. Vincent at Le Mans, St. Martin at Séez, St. Mary's at Nevers, and even by more distant foundations, St. Peter's at Lyons and the great Abbey of St. Germain des Prés at Paris. One point of the new practice, that Abbots should be elected for only three years at a time, struck at the prevailing abuse by which members of powerful families, non-resident and often children, were intruded into rich benefices, to the great detriment of their charges.[1] Consideration was also had of the rule adopted at St. Justina's at Padua,

[1] Thus the family of d'Illiers at this time almost monopolized the see of Chartres; members of it holding the bishopric consecutively for fifty years, the deanery for a hundred, the archdeaconry and the rich abbey of Bona Vallis also for fifty.

the centre of reform in Northern Italy; and thus it was not till 1516 that the new ordinances were finally sanctioned by Leo x.

About 1490, Jouveneaux, fired with enthusiasm by the success of du Mas' reforms at Chezal Benoît, determined to quit his professor's chair at Paris and take upon him the vows and the life of a monk under du Mas' rule; and subsequently he was the means of bringing into the Congregation the Abbey of St. Sulpice at Bourges, being invited thither by John Labat, the Abbot, to introduce the new rule, and himself succeeding to the abbacy for a triennial period. A year or two after his retirement from the world, he was followed to Chezal Benoît by Charles Fernand, who subsequently went on to St. Vincent's at Le Mans. John Fernand also ended his days at St. Sulpice in Bourges.

Charles Fernand is a personality who deserves more attention than he has received. Whilst he was in the world he enjoyed considerable esteem amongst the learned. He was a friend of Gaguin, and published a commentary on Gaguin's poem on the Immaculate Conception; he also dedicated to Gaguin a small volume of Familiar Letters. But his most important literary work was done in the retirement of his cell: a volume of Monastic Conversations, composed at sundry times, and published in 1516; a treatise on Tranquillity (1512), in which he gives an account of the motives which led him to take the monastic habit; and a Mirror of the Monastic Life (1515), dwelling at length on the ideals that should be held before the eyes of novices and animate their lives when they were professed. Unfortunately his style is so excessively elegant, with wide intervals between words closely connected in sense, that he is difficult to read; and hence, perhaps, in some measure the neglect which has been meted out to him.

Of his four Monastic Conversations the first and the last are concerned with the question whether monks should be allowed to read the books of the Gentiles, that is to say, the classics. He handles his theme sensibly and liberally. Piety, of course, is to come before eloquence, and there is to be choice of books. Anything of loose tendency is to be forbidden, but he would encourage the reading of Cicero, Seneca, and Aristotle's Ethics. The last was only accessible to himself, he says regretfully, in Latin, because he knew no Greek—a loss which he greatly deplores, desiring to read the Greek Fathers. The third conversation is about the Benedictine rule, directed to the lawless monks who contended that they were only bound by the customs of the particular monastery they had entered, and not by the general ordinances of their founder. He combats at length the contention that the world has grown old, and that latter-day men cannot be expected to undergo the rigorous fasts and penances achieved by St. Antony and St. Benedict. He is quite alive to the weakness of the age, to the need for improvement in the monasteries; and the word Reformer is applied with praise to the leaders of the movement.

This was before the days of Luther, though only just before.

Incidentally, an argument is reported between a Christian and an agnostic. After their diverse opinions have been rehearsed, the Christian concludes with what is meant to be a crushing reply—certainly it silences his opponent: 'On your own theory you don't know what will happen after death. On mine you will prosper, if you believe; if not, you will go to hell. Therefore safety lies in believing mine.'

There are one or two glimpses of the life of the monks. At the end of one conversation, the other brother hears the bell ringing for prayers and runs off to chapel; Fernand, being old and lame, will be forgiven if he is a little late, and not fined of his dinner. In other ways consideration was shown to him, and he was often sent to dine in the infirmary, not being expected with his toothless jaws to munch the dry crusts set before the rest of the house. This, it seems, was a custom which had been learnt from St. Justina's at Padua, to put out the stale crusts first, before the new bread, to break appetite upon: just as in the old Quaker schools a hundred years ago, children were set down to suet-pudding, and then broth, before the joint appeared; the order being, 'No ball, no broth; no broth, no beef'.

We are in a position to view from the inside another Benedictine house at this period, that of Ottobeuren, near Memmingen, which lies about midway between Augsburg and the east end of the Lake of Constance. The source of our information is the correspondence of one of the brothers, Nicholas Ellenbog (or Cubitus); 890 letters copied out in his own hand, and only 80 of these printed. It is not so continuous a narrative as Butzbach's, but the picture that it gives is rather more pleasing.

Nicholas' father was Ulrich Ellenbog, a physician of Memmingen, who graduated as Doctor of Medicine from Pavia in 1459, and became first Reader in Medicine at Ingolstadt. The letters introduce us to most of his children. One son, Onofrius, went for a soldier, became attached to Maximilian's train, and received a knighthood; another, Ulrich, became M.D. at Siena, but died immediately afterwards; another, John, became a parish priest. Of the daughters three remained in the world; one, Elizabeth, married; another, Cunigunde, died of plague caught in nursing some nuns. The fourth daughter, Barbara, at the age of nine entered the convent of Heppach, and lived there forty-one years, rising to be Prioress and then Abbess. We shall hear of her again.

Nicholas Ellenbog, 1480 or 1481–1543, was the third son. After five years at Heidelberg, 1497–1502, in which he met Wimpfeling and was fellow-student, though a year senior, to Oecolampadius, he went off to Cracow, the Polish university, which was then so flourishing as to attract students from the west. Schurer, for example, the Strasburg printer, was M.A. of Cracow in 1494; and some idea of the condition of learning there may be gained from a bookseller's letter to Aldus from Cracow, December 1505, ordering 100 copies of Constantine Lascaris' Greek grammar. For some months Ellenbog heard lectures there on astronomy, which remained a favourite subject with him throughout his life. Then an impulse came to him to follow his father's footsteps in medicine, and at the advice of friends he went back across half Europe to Montpellier, which from its earliest days had been famous for its medical faculty. In the long vacation of 1502 he spent two months with a friend in the château of a nobleman among the Gascon hills, and on their return journey they stayed for a fortnight in a house of Dominican nuns. The sisters were strict in their observances, and gave a good pattern of the unworldly life, which attracted Ellenbog strongly. In 1503 he went home for the long vacation to Memmingen. On the way he was taken by the plague, and with difficulty dragged himself in to Ravensburg. For three months he lay ill, and death came very close. As its unearthly glow irradiated the world around him, reversing its light and shade, the visions of the nunnery recurred. He vowed that if his life were still his to give, it should be given to God's service; and on recovering he entered Ottobeuren.

In his noviciate year he was under the guidance of a kind and sympathetic novice-master, who allowed him to study quietly in his cell to his heart's content; and during this period he composed what he calls an epitome or breviary of Plato. Its precise character he does not specify, but its second title suggests that it may have been a collection of extracts from

Plato: not from the Greek, for he had little acquaintance with that yet, but presumably from such of Plato's works as had been translated into Latin. On Ascension Day, 1504, which appears from other indications to mean 15 August, he made his profession, and in September 1505 he went to Augsburg to be ordained as sub-deacon. Writing to a friend to give such news as he had gathered on this outing, he tells a story to convict himself of hasty judgement. During the ordination service he noticed that one of the candidates, a bold-eyed fellow who had been at several universities, and had been Rector at Siena, let his gaze wander over the ladies who had come to see the ceremony, instead of keeping it fixed on the altar. Ellenbog censured him in his mind, but later he noticed that as the man kneeled before the bishop with folded hands to receive unction, his eyes were filled with tears of repentance—others perhaps would have called it merely emotion.

On his way back to Ottobeuren, Ellenbog arrived at a village, where he had counted on a night's rest, only to find it crowded with a wedding-party; the followers of the bridegroom, who were escorting him to the marriage on the morrow, a Sunday. It was with great difficulty that he found shelter, in the house of a cobbler, who let him sleep with his family in the straw; but it was so uncomfortable that before dawn he crept out and started on his way under the moon. In the half light he missed the road and found himself at the bride's castle; where he learnt that her sister was just dead and the wedding postponed. As he passed in that evening through the abbey-gate, there was thankfulness in his heart that he was back out of the world and its petty disappointments.

On Low Sunday, 1506, he was ordained priest at Ottobeuren, and celebrated his first mass. Some of his letters are to friends inviting them to be present, and adjuring them to come empty-handed, without the customary gifts. In these early years there was ample leisure for study. In 1505 he began Greek, and in 1508 Hebrew. He speaks of reading Aeneas Sylvius, Pico della Mirandola, Cyprian, Diogenes Laertius, Ambrose, Chrysostom, Dionysius the Areopagite. He went on with his astronomy, and cast horoscopes for his friends. Binding books was one of his occupations; and in 1509, when a press was set up in the monastery, he lent a hand in the printing. He was very fortunate in his abbot, Leonard Widemann, who had been Steward when he entered Ottobeuren, but was elected Abbot in 1508, and outlived him by three years, dying in 1546. Widemann called upon him for service. Immediately on election he made him Prior—at 28—and only released him from this office after four years, to make him, though infinitely reluctant, serve ten years more as Steward.

But if the Abbot knew how to exact compliance, he knew also how to reward. He gave Ellenbog every assistance in his studies, allowed him to write hither and thither for books, made continual efforts to procure him first a Hebrew and then a Greek

Bible, wrote to Reuchlin to find him a converted Jew as Hebrew teacher, and in 1516 built him a new library; for which Ellenbog writes to a friend asking for verses to put under the paintings of the Doctors of the Church, which are to adorn the walls. As results of his studies we hear of him correcting the abbey service-books, where for *stauros*, a scribe with no Greek had written *scayros*, and explaining to the Abbot mistaken interpretations in the passages read aloud in the refectory during meals. One of these, in a book written by some one who had recently been canonized—some mediaeval doctor—illustrates the learning of the day; deriving γαστριμαργία, gluttony, from *castrum* and *mergo*, 'quod gula mergat castrum mentis,' because gluttony drowns the seat of reason.

Of Ellenbog's official duties occasional mention is made in his letters. As Steward he has to visit the tenants of the monastery; in the autumn he journeys about the country buying wine. We hear of him at Westerhaim, on the river Iller, settling a dispute among the fishermen. On one of his journeys to fetch wine from Constance, at the hospice there he fell in with a man who could fire balls out of a machine by means of nitre, and who boasted that he could demolish with this weapon a certain castle in the neighbourhood. Over supper they began to argue, the artillerist maintaining that nitre was cold, and that the explosion which discharged the balls was caused by the contrariety between nitre and sulphur; Ellenbog contending that nitre was hot, and supporting this view by scraps remembered from his father's scientific conversation.

The general life of the Abbey is also reflected. Ottobeuren lay on one of the routes to Italy, and so they had plenty of visitors bringing news from regions far off: a Carthusian, who had been in Ireland and seen St. Patrick's cave; a party of Hungarian acrobats with dancing bears; a young Cretan, John Bondius, who had seen the labyrinth of Minos, but all walled up to prevent men from straying into it and being lost. A great impression he made, when he dined with the Abbot; he was so learned and polished, and spoke Latin so well for a Greek. In 1514 Pellican, the Franciscan Visitor, passed on his way south, and had a talk with Ellenbog, which was all too short, about Hebrew learning. Next year came Eck, the theologian, the future champion of orthodoxy, returning from Rome. Eck's mother and sisters were living under the protection of the abbey—it is not clear whether they were merely tenants, or whether they were occupying lay quarters within its walls, as did Fernand's at St. Germain's in Paris. At any rate, Eck came and made himself agreeable. He preached twice before the brethren; and when he left, he promised to send them the latest news from America. In 1511 a copy of Vespucci's narrative of his voyage had been lent to the monastery, and had been read with great interest.

A grave question arose whether the new races discovered in the West were to be accounted as saved or damned. Ellenbog quotes Faber Stapulensis' statement that nothing could be more bestial than the condition of the Indians whom da Gama had discovered in 1498 in Calicut, Cannanore, and Ceylon; it was to be feared that the Indians of the West were no better. In writing to Ellenbog six months later to say that he had no clear opinions on the question, Eck uses an interesting expression: 'To ask what I think is like looking for Arthur and his Britons.'[1] The reference is to the Arthurian legend and the long-expected, never-fulfilled, return of the great king; but the humanists usually leave the whole field of mediaeval romance severely alone.

One September morning, when the dew was still heavy, Ellenbog went out with some brethren to gather apples. At the top of the orchard[2] one of them called out that he had found 'a star'. It was a damp white deposit on the grass, clammy and quivering, cold to the touch, very sticky, with long tenacious filaments. Ellenbog had never seen anything like it, but he found out that the peasants and the shepherds believed such things to be droppings from shooting stars,[3] if not actually fallen stars, and that they were thought to be a cure for cancer. His letter describing it is to ask the opinion of a friend who was a doctor, that is to say, the scientist of the age.

The affairs of Ellenbog's family often appear. His

[1] Arcturum cum Britannis exspectatis. For another allusion to Arthur, see Pace, *De Fructu*, p. 83.

[2] ortus.

[3] stellae emuncturam et purgamentum.

father had been a great collector of books, which he had corrected with his own hand, and which at his death he had wished to be kept together as a common heirloom for the whole family. A great many of them were medical, and therefore it had seemed good that the enjoyment of the books should go to Ulrich, the son who was studying medicine at Siena. On his way home, after completing his course, Ulrich died; and Nicholas composed a piteous appeal on behalf of the books, bewailing their fate that after ten years of confinement their hope of being used had come to nothing. Onofrius was the only brother from whom might be hoped a younger generation of Ellenbogs, one of whom might study medicine. Elizabeth's children were Geslers, and so apparently did not count.

How long the books were kept together is not known. One of them is now in the University Library at Cambridge, and has been excellently described in an essay by the late Robert Proctor. It consists of several volumes bound together: Henry of Rimini on the Cardinal Virtues, the Journey of a penitent soul through Lent, a treatise *de diuina predestinacione*, and John Peckham, Archbishop of Canterbury, *de oculo morali*—all of a definitely religious or moral character. They are freely annotated by the father's hand, with marginalia which throw light on his life and times, his dislike of the Venetians for their anti-papal policy, his experiences as physician to the Abbey of St. Ulrich in Augsburg, and the part that he played in the introduction of printing there. On Lady Day, 1481, shortly after Nicholas' birth, perhaps when he had lived just a week and seemed likely to thrive, the father composed an address to his four living sons —four being already dead—, and wrote it into this volume. He adjures them to follow learning and goodness, and finally bids them take every care of the books, and not let them be separated. This it was which inspired Nicholas' appeal thirty years later, when Ulrich, the son, was cut off, just as his eyes seemed about to follow his father's up and down the pages.

Ellenbog's letters to his sister Barbara are amusing. She was four or five years older than he, but being a woman had not had his opportunities. He begins by trying to teach her Latin. But the difficulties were many, and apparently she did not progress far enough to write in the tongue. At any rate, Ellenbog copied none of her letters into his book; a fact which is to be deplored both from her point of view and from ours. One would like to know what reply she made to some of his homilies. She invited him once to come and see her at Heppach, with leave from her Abbess. He replies cautiously that, if he comes, he hopes they will be able to talk without being overheard; for Onofrius had been once, and when he made a rather coarse remark, there had been giggles outside the door. In 1512 Barbara became Prioress, and Ellenbog took the opportunity to lecture her at length upon spiritual pride and the importance of humility;

sweetening his dose of virtue with a present of cinnamon, ginger, and nutmeg.

Once she let fall some regrets that she had brought nothing into her convent, and was dependent on it for food and clothing; evidently she would have liked some share of the patrimony which had been divided between her married sisters and the brothers who remained in the world. Nicholas' reply was that Heppach, like other monasteries, was well endowed; she had given herself, and that was quite enough. In 1515 Barbara was elected Abbess; and received another discourse about spiritual pride. John and Elizabeth wrote to Nicholas saying that they had been invited to Heppach to salute the new Reverend Mother, and suggesting that he should come too. But his plain speaking had had its reward, no invitation had come for him. Under the circumstances, he writes, he could not think of going; besides he had been there several times before, and had found it very dull; it was clearly John's duty to go, as he had not been once in twenty years, although his parish was only three miles from Heppach. However the breach was healed, and a proper invitation came for Nicholas; but the business of his stewardship prevented him from accepting.

The relations with John, the parish priest of Wurtzen, are more harmonious. There is a frequent exchange of presents, John sending tools for wood-carving, and crayfish; which seem to have been common in his neighbourhood, for Nicholas occasionally asks for them. The only lecture is one passed on from Barbara. John had been created a chaplain to Maximilian, an honorific title, with few or no duties; and Barbara had feared that he might neglect the flock in his parish. On another occasion Nicholas urges him to follow Elizabeth's advice, and get an unmarried man to be his housekeeper. He had proposed to have a man with a family; and Elizabeth was afraid for his reputation. John was a frequent guest at Ottobeuren, and one of Nicholas' invitations contains what is unusual among the humanists, an appreciation of the charms of the country: 'Come,' he says, 'and hear the songs of the birds, the shepherds' pipes and the children's horns, the choruses of reapers and ploughmen, and the voices of the girls as they work in the fields.'

By his younger relatives, Ellenbog did his duty unfailingly. Elizabeth's eldest son, John Gesler, was at school at Memmingen. When a new schoolmaster was appointed, Ellenbog wrote to bespeak his interest in the boy, and to suggest the books that he should read: Donatus' Grammar and the letters of Filelfo. At 14 he persuaded the parents to send John to Heidelberg, and took a great deal of trouble in arranging that the boy should be lodged with his own teacher, Peter of Wimpina. When two years later Elizabeth grew anxious about John's health and proposed to take him with her to some of the numerous baths, which then as now abounded in Germany and Switzerland, it was again

Nicholas who made the arrangements; and in 1515, when John had left Heidelberg, Nicholas proposed to exchange letters with him daily, in order that he might not forget his Latin. In January 1515 Elizabeth's eldest daughter, Barbara, was married to a certain Conrad Ankaryte. In December 1530 he writes to one of the nuns at Heppach to announce that he has persuaded two girls, the children of this marriage, to embrace the religious life. The elder, Anna, aged 13, was forward with her education, as she was well acquainted with German literature and was reading Latin with her father [1]; by the following summer she would be ready to come to Heppach. For the younger, who was not yet 7, he begged a few years' grace, though she was eager to come at once. Truly children developed earlier in those days.

The happiest time of Ellenbog's life began in the summer of 1522, when after ten years' service he was allowed by the Abbot to resign his Stewardship. His accounts were audited satisfactorily, and he was discharged, to what seemed to him a riotous banquet of leisure. 'In the quiet of my cell,' he wrote to his brother, 'I read, I write, I meditate, I pray, I paint, I carve'. His interest in astronomy was resumed, and he set himself to make dials for pocket use, on metal rings or on round wooden sticks. The latter he turned for himself upon a lathe; and

[1] quae legere literas vernaculae linguae satis expedite nouit, nunc per patrem imbuitur Latinis.

for this work John sent him a present of boxwood, juniper, and plane. By the New Year of 1523 he had made two sundials; one which showed the time on five sides at once, he sent to John at Wurtzen, the other to Barbara at Heppach. His cell looked South, and thus he could study the movements of the moon and the planets, and note the southing of the stars. He could turn his skill to profit, too, and exchange his dials for pictures of the saints.

In 1525 his peace was broken by the Peasants' Revolt, which swept like a hurricane over South Germany. Hostility to religion was not one of its moving causes, but the monks were vulnerable, and had always been considered fair game, especially by local nobles whom in the plenitude of their power they had not troubled to conciliate. The peasants of the Rhine valley had not forgotten the burning of Limburg, near Spires, by William of Hesse in 1504. The abbey church had scarcely a rival in Germany, and the flames burned for twelve days. With such an example, and with their prey unresisting, the peasants were not likely to stay their hands. At Freiburg they brought to his death Gregory Reisch, the learned Carthusian Prior of St. Johannisberg, the friend of Maximilian. Ellenbog enumerates four monasteries burned in his neighbourhood during the outbreak—three by the peasants incensed against their landlords, and one by a noble who bore it a grudge. When the first attack came in April, Ellenbog was staying at the monastery of St. George, at Isny, about twenty miles away. The peasants there destroyed everything belonging to the monks that they could find outside the walls, and threatened dire treatment when they should force their way in; but mercifully the walls were strong, and held out.

Ottobeuren was less fortunate. Being in the country, it had to rely upon itself, and so fell an easy prey. The buildings were defaced, the windows broken, the stoves and ovens wrecked, and all the ironwork carried off. Scarcely a door remained on its hinges, and the furniture of the rooms disappeared. The church was violated, its pictures soiled, and its statues smashed; Christ's wounds should be wounds indeed, hard voices cried, as axe and hammer rung over their pitiless work. The library was emptied of its books. Walls and roofs and floors were all that the monks found when they ventured back. Ellenbog, however, fared better than many. A friendly brother had seized up some of his books and papers and hidden them in the clock-tower; and the abbey carpenter thinking this insecure had found them better cover, presumably in his own house. The tempest over, calm soon returned. The countryfolk, many of whom had remained friendly, began bringing back spoil which they had wrested from wrongful possessors. Some of Ellenbog's books were brought in; and as much as two years later he recovered one of his astronomical instruments. He lost, however, a number of his father's papers, which he had been on the point of editing; a Hebrew Bible given to him by

Onofrius; and the first two books of his collection of his own letters. 'God knows whether they will ever come back,' he wrote at the beginning of the third book; and to him they never did. They are now safe at Stuttgart, though in permanent divorce from the other seven books, which are in Paris.

Ellenbog was no coward. In the autumn the vineyards belonging to the Abbey were to be inspected, and the due tithes of wine exacted. Unless this were done the monks would suffer lack; so some one had to be sent, in spite of the last mutterings of the revolt. One vineyard lay at Immenstadt, some distance to the South, and thus Ellenbog at Isny was already part way thither. Moreover, having served as Steward, he would know what was required. The Abbot sent down a horse and bade him go: though the roads were held by armed outlaws, who were reported to be specially hostile to monks. He was afraid; but he summoned his courage and went. If the Abbey seemed a haven before, when he came back to it from the experiences of his ordination at Augsburg, this time it was a refuge and strength against the fear that lurketh in forests and the imagination of pursuing footsteps.

IV

UNIVERSITIES

In the autumn of 1495 Erasmus was at length at liberty to go to a university. His patron, the Bishop of Cambray, gave him a small allowance, and the authorities at Steyn were prevailed upon to consent. His purpose was to obtain a Doctor's degree in Theology; and so he entered the College of Montaigu at Paris, which had been founded in 1388, but had fallen into decay and only recently been revived. In 1483 a certain John Standonck had volunteered to become Principal. By his efforts the college buildings were restored; and by taking in rich pupils he secured means to maintain the Domus Pauperum attached to the College. He was an ardent, enthusiastic person, but rather lacking in judgement; and starved his *pauperes* in order to be able to have as many as possible on the slender resources available. Erasmus, being delicate and therewith fastidious, complained of the rough and meagre fare—rotten eggs and stinking water; and with good reason, for it made him ill, and he had to spend the summer of 1496 with his friends in Holland.

Having established himself in the college he introduced himself to the literary circle in Paris, through its head, Robert Gaguin, the aged General of the Maturins, who had served on many embassies, to Spain, to Italy, to Germany, to England. Gaguin had written much himself, and had been one of the promoters of printing in Paris. To know him was to be known of many. Erasmus began by addressing to him a poem and some florid letters, and showed him some of his work. Then an opportunity came to do him a service. Gaguin had composed a history of the French, and it was just coming through the press. At the end the printer found himself with two pages of the last sheet unfilled, despite ample spacing out, and the author was too ill to lend any help. Erasmus heard of the difficulty, and came to the rescue with a long and most elegant epistle to Gaguin, comparing him to Sallust and Livy, and promising him immortality. Time has turned the tables: Gaguin's name lives, not because of his history, but because the young and unknown Augustinian canon thought fit to court his acquaintance.

Once blooded with the printers, Erasmus went steadily on. In a few months he published some poems of his own, on Christ and the angels—*de casa natalitia Jesu*, a very rare volume, of which only two copies are known. It was dedicated to a college friend, Hector Boys, of Dundee, subsequently the first Principal of King's College, Aberdeen, and historian of Scotland. It may be wondered what was Erasmus' motive. A dedication of a book had a market value and usually brought a return in proportion to the compliments laid on. Correctness certainly required that the book should be sent to the Bishop of Cambray. Boys was only a fellow-student, whose acquaintance Erasmus had made at

Montaigu. The explanation perhaps lies in the fact that Bishop Elphinstone was then negotiating with Boys to come to Aberdeen; in the newly-founded university Erasmus may have sighted hopes for himself. The following year saw another volume produced by him; the poems of his Gouda and Deventer friend, William Herman, with a few of his own added. This time the Bishop of Cambray did not fail of his due.

When Erasmus came to Paris, he was nearly 29, older by far than the ordinary arts student, but not old for the theological course, which lasted longer than the others. To reach the first step, the Bachelor's degree, he had to attend a number of lectures; and very tedious he found them. Theologians are apt to be conservative. The method of instruction had not advanced far beyond the dictation of text and gloss and commentary, which had been current before the days of printing. Erasmus yawned and dozed, or wrote letters to his friends making fun of these 'barbarous Scotists'. 'You wouldn't know me,' he says, 'if you could see me sitting under old Dunderhead, my brows knit and looking thoroughly puzzled. They tell me that no one can understand these mysteries who has any traffic with the Muses or the Graces. So I am trying hard to forget my Latin: wit and elegance must disappear. I think I am getting on; maybe some day they will recognize me for their own.' They did, and he proceeded B.D.; when is not known, but probably by Easter 1498.

At the present day in England our systems are very set. A man matriculates at a university and completes his course there: to change even from one college to another is becoming almost unknown. Abroad, however, things are more fluid, and students pass on from university to university in search of the best teacher for special parts of their course. So it was in Erasmus' time. A course of lectures attended in one university could be reckoned in another; and thus men often proceeded to their degrees within a short time of their matriculation. Having taken his Bachelor's degree at Paris, Erasmus at once proposed to convert it into a Doctor's in Italy; but one hope after another of going there was disappointed. In 1506 he wished to take it in Cambridge; but after obtaining his grace, he was offered a chance to go to Italy as tutor to the sons of Henry VII's Italian physician. He accepted with delight, and was made D.D. as he passed through Turin; the formalities apparently requiring only a few days.

The art of reasoning is an excellent thing; and so long as man continues to live according to reason, some training in this art will continue to be a part of education. Indeed, an elementary knowledge of it is as necessary as an elementary acquaintance with the art of arithmetic. Both arts have this in common that though their feet walk upon the earth, their heads are lost in the clouds. A moderate attainment of them is indispensable to all; but their higher developments can only be comprehended by the acutest minds. In the Middle Ages the art of reasoning had been raised to such a pitch of perfection that it entirely dominated the schools. Its exponents were so proud of it that its bounds were continually extended; and it became impossible to obtain a university degree without a high level of proficiency in disputation. For his examination a candidate was required to dispute with all comers—in practice this came to be a small number of appointed examiners, three or four—on questions which had been announced beforehand. It was not a hasty affair—time was allowed for reflection, and the examination might easily last several hours or even all day. But clearly readiness in debate was likely to count in a man's favour, and so besides knowledge of standard authors to be adduced in support of opinions—the Bible, the Fathers, the mediaeval commentators, the Canon Law and the glosses upon it—it was important to a candidate to be able to handle a question properly, to divide it up into its different parts by means of distinctions, to shear off side issues, to examine the various facets which it presented when approached from different points of view; and all this without hesitation, and of course in Latin.

In order to train candidates in this art, university and college teachers gave frequent exhibitions of disputations, which from being on any subject, de quolibet, were styled 'quodlibeticae questiones', or 'disputationes'. A high dignitary presided, with the title of 'dominus quodlibetarius', and propounded questions, usually one supported by arguments and two plain; and then the disputer, who presumably came prepared, delivered his reply, clear cut into fine distinctions and bristling with citations from recognized authorities. Such work necessarily cost trouble and forethought, and the hard-working teacher of the day, instead of printing his lectures on philosophy or history or editing and commentating texts, gave to his pupils in permanent form the quodlibetical disputations which the busy among them had struggled to copy down into note-books, and over which the inattentive, like Erasmus, had yawned.

These are some of the subjects disputed at Louvain, 1488–1507, by Adrian of Utrecht; first as a young doctor, then as professor of theology, and finally for ten years as vice-chancellor, before he was carried away to become tutor to Prince Charles, and entered upon the public career which led him finally to Rome as Adrian VI.

1488. Whether to avoid offending one's neighbour it is permissible to break a vow or oath duly made.

1491. Whether one is bound to act on the command of a superior, contrary to one's own opinion, knowing that in former days the matter had been regarded as doubtful.

1492. Whether it is lawful to administer the Eucharist or to confer the benefit of absolution on one who declares that he cannot abstain from crimes.

1493. Whether of the two is more likely to be healed and offends God the less, the man who sins from ignorance or infirmity, or the man who sins of deliberate intent.

1495. Whether a priest who gives advice that tithes ought not to be paid on the fruits of one's own labours, can receive remission of his sin without undergoing severe punishment.

Whether transgression of human laws constitutes mortal sin.

1499. Whether prayer on behalf of many is as beneficial to the individuals as if one prayed as long a time for each one.

1491. Whether it is permissible to give money to
⟨? 1501⟩ any one to procure one a benefice by praising one's dignity and merits to the provisor to the benefice.

Here are some of John Briard of Ath, a notable theologian, who was subsequently Vice-chancellor of Louvain:

1508. Whether a man who has confessed all his mortal sins but has omitted his voluntary occasions of stumbling, is bound to confess over again.

Whether we are bound by the law of love to deliver a neighbour, against his will, from oppression, infamy, or death, when we cannot do so without hurt or danger to ourselves.

Whether beneficed students on account of their studies are excused from reading their canonical hours.

We will now consider in brief Briard's handling of the following question: 'Whether a prize of money won at Bruges or elsewhere by the hazard known as the game of the pot, or what is commonly called the lottery, may be retained with a clear conscience as a righteous acquisition?'

'For the decision of this question I premise:

1. Firstly, that gain is not to be considered unlawful because it comes by good fortune, and not by one's own labour.

   The truth of this preamble is shown thus: If gain coming by good fortune is unlawful, it follows that all gain arising from division by lot is unlawful. But this is false: therefore, &c.

   The consequent is proved by the fact that all such gain rests on good fortune. The falsity is shown by the opinions of almost all the doctors who write on this subject:

   St. Thomas, 2.2, question 95, article 8, shows that there is nothing wrong in dividing by lot, between friends who cannot otherwise decide.

   In this opinion agree Alexander of Hales, part 2 of his *Summa*, question 185, membrane 2; Angelus in his *Summa* under the word *sors*, section 2, after the gloss in *Summa* 26, question 2; Antoninus, part 2, title 12, chapter 1, section 9.

2. Secondly, that gain is not to be considered unlawful because it comes without labour.

   This would exclude gifts.

3. Thirdly, that gain is not to be considered unlawful because it comes from cupidity, avarice, forbidden trade, or opus peccaminosum ⟨e.g. working on a saint's day⟩, unless there is fraud, deception, or the like.

See Petrus de Palude, book 4, distinction 15, question 3, conclusion 4, about the gain arising from acting. Also Angelus in his *Summa* under *restitutio*, part 1, section 6.

4. Fourthly, that a work which brings public advantage, either spiritual or temporal, is not necessarily unlawful because some people are thereby provoked to sin.

Otherwise it would be unlawful to manufacture arms or to make war.

On these premises I base the following propositions:

1. The lottery is not in itself unlawful.

Proof. It is not prohibited by any law, divine, human, or natural: divine, because it is not forbidden in Scripture; human, because there is no law against it as there is against hazard or dicing; natural, because it is not excluded as (*a*) coming by good fortune, (*b*) provoking others to sin, (*c*) vain and useless.

a and *b* are proved by premiss 1 and 4. *c* is proved because we are supposing that the lottery is undertaken in order that the city of Bruges may make a profit with which to pay off some of its municipal debt, or be lightened of some of its common burdens, so that its citizens may be free to journey whither they please. (That this last refers among other things to pilgrimage, may be inferred from a reference to the Canon Law on the undertaking of journeys, chapter on Sacred Churches.)

2. The lottery is not prohibited by the human laws forbidding hazard and dice.

Proof. The laws prohibiting these do not forbid the lottery, nor can it be included under them by parity of reasoning. For hazard is not forbidden because it depends on chance, or else all gaming would be forbidden ; and it is not forbidden to play for small stakes or on the occasion of a party. But it (hazard) is forbidden because, as Petrus de Palude says in book 4, distinction 15, question 3, article 5, the person who loses is wont to blaspheme; and also because men are tempted to lose more than they can afford.'

We need not follow the argument in detail, but the fourth proposition is interesting, 'That there is an injustice in the lotteries as practised by some cities, in that the creditors of the city are compelled against their will to take part in the lottery, and so probably make a loss, for fear of not recovering the money owed to them'. After six propositions come two contrary arguments, which are refuted by five and two considerations; and then there is a brief summing up.

Excellent reasoning this doubtless was, and the

student who could dispute over these intricacies for hours together, must have had at least a competent knowledge of Latin, understanded of the examiners; but it is not surprising that the humanists desired something better.

The universities did not live upon the teaching of the colleges alone. Scholars came from abroad and competed with the home-bred talent to supply such private tuition as was required, and when their ability had been proved, received licence from the university to teach publicly. The advantage generally rested with the new-comer. *Omne ignotum pro mirifico.* When there was so much to learn, so much novelty that the stranger might bring with him, it was little wonder that a new arrival aroused excitement, especially if he came with a reputation. Teachers travelled from one university to another in search of employment, and any one with a knowledge of Greek or Hebrew was sure to find pupils and attentive audiences. So great was the enthusiasm on both sides, that lectures often lasted for hours.

Aleander, when he returned from Orleans to Paris in 1511, kept quiet for a month, in order to awaken public interest. Then he announced a course of lectures on Ausonius, to begin on 30 July. His device was entirely successful. Two thousand people gathered, and he was obliged to lead them over from his own college, de la Marche, to a larger building, known as the Portico of Cambray. He had composed an elaborate oration of twenty-four pages. 'It took me two hours and a half to deliver,' he says, 'and would have taken four, if I hadn't been a quick reader; but no one showed the least sign of fatigue, in spite of the heat. My voice lasted very well. Next day I had nearly as good an audience, although it was the day for the disputation at the Sorbonne. On the day after, all seats were taken by 11, though I do not begin till 1.' His success was not mere imagination. One who was present tells us that men looked upon him as if he had come down from heaven, and shouted 'Viuat, viuat', as they were accustomed to do to Faustus Andrelinus, another witty Italian who was then lecturing in Paris. A lecturer to-day who went on into the third hour would scarcely be so popular.

But Aleander was not alone in his powers of speech, and others besides Parisians could listen. Butzbach tells us, not without humour, of a certain Baldwin Bessel of Haarlem, a learned physician with a wonderful memory, who was summoned to Laach to heal their Abbot, who lay sick. On one occasion at Coblenz he harangued an audience of 300 for three hours on end on the power of eloquence, and stimulated by the sight of such a gathering, worked himself up in his peroration, until he believed himself to be a second Cicero. His hearers perhaps did not agree. Anyway, Butzbach is the only person who mentions him, and he would have preferred a little less eloquence and a little more medicine; for the Abbot, instead of recovering, died under the hands of the new Cicero in two days.

Besides lecturing at the university, young men also maintained themselves by working for the printers, correcting proof-sheets and composing complimentary prefaces and verses. Another service which they could render to both printers and authors was to give public 'interpretations', as they were called, of new books on publication, for the purpose of advertisement. These interpretations probably took place at the printer's office, and were of the nature of a review, describing the book's contents; and they were doubtless repeated at frequent intervals before new groups of likely purchasers.

Erasmus, however, had been sent to Paris to take a degree in Theology, and his patrons expected him to occupy himself with this. When he returned from Holland in 1496 he could not face again the rigours of Montaigu, and so he took shelter in a boarding-house kept by a termagant woman—a 'pessima mulier' the bursar of the German nation, her landlords, called her when she would not pay her rent—, the wife of a minor court official. So long as his supplies lasted, he kept strictly to his work; but when the Bishop failed him, he was obliged to support himself, and took to private teaching. Two of his pupils were young men from Lubeck, who were under the care of a teacher from their own part of the world, Augustine Vincent, a budding scholar, who afterwards published an edition of Virgil, but who as yet was glad to be helped by Erasmus. Another pair came from England, one a kinsman of

John Fisher, and were in the charge of a morose North-countryman. In great poverty, Erasmus made his way somehow, occasionally writing little treatises for his pupils, on a method of study, on letter-writing—an important art in those days—, a paraphrase of the *Elegantiae* of Valla; and finally, one of his best-known works, the Colloquies, had its origin in a little composition of this period, which he refers to as 'sermones quosdam quotidianos quibus in congressibus et conuiuiis vtimur'—a few formulas of address and expressions of polite sentiments, which develop into brief conversations.

The poor scholar's hardships were mitigated by the generosity of a friend. Whilst with the Bishop of Cambray Erasmus had made the acquaintance of a young man from Bergen-op-Zoom, the Bishop's ancestral home; one James Batt, who after education in Paris had returned to be master of the public school in his native town. About 1498 Batt was engaged as private tutor to the son of Anne of Borsselen, widow of an Admiral of Flanders and hereditary Lady of Veere, an important sea-port town in Walcheren which then did much trade with Scotland, and whose great, dumb cathedral and ornate town-hall still tell to the handful of houses round them the story of former greatness. From the first Batt applied himself to win his patroness' favour to his clever and needy friend. Erasmus was invited to visit them, money was sent for his journey; and within a short time he was receiving pecuniary contributions from the Lady more frequently than if she had been allowing him a pension. His letters to Batt—the replies which came he never published—are remarkable reading, and do credit to both sides. Conscious of high powers and pressed by urgent need, Erasmus begins by begging without concealment, for money to keep him going and give him leisure. But as time goes on and the Lady wearies of much giving, Erasmus' tone grows sharper and more insistent; until at last he scolds and upbraids his patient correspondent for not extorting more, and even bids him put his own needs in the background until Erasmus' are satisfied. Batt's name deserves to be remembered as chief amongst faithful friends, for putting up with such scant gratitude after his inexhaustible devotion; and we must needs think more highly of Erasmus, if his friend could accept such treatment at his hand and not be wounded. To the great much littleness may be forgiven. The surprising thing is that Erasmus should have allowed such letters to be published.

In the summer of 1499 Erasmus was carried off to England by another friend whom he had captivated, the young Lord Mountjoy, who had come abroad to study until the child-bride whom he had already married should be old enough to become his wife. After a summer spent among bright-eyed English ladies at a country-house in Hertfordshire, then studded with the hunting-boxes of the nobility, and a visit to London which brought him into quick friendship with More, ten or eleven years his junior, Erasmus persuaded his patron to take him for a while to Oxford. Mountjoy promised but could not perform. The Earl of Warwick was to be tried in Westminster Hall, and Mountjoy as a peer must be in his place. So Erasmus rode in to Oxford, over Shotover and across Milham ford, alone.

As an Austin canon he had a claim on St. Mary's, a college which had been established in 1435 at the instance of a number of Augustinian abbots and priors, for the purpose of bringing young canons to Oxford to profit by the life and studies of the university; in much the same way that Mansfield and Manchester Colleges have joined us in recent years. For two or three months he was here, enjoying the society of the learned and attending Colet's lectures on the Epistles of St. Paul; invited to dine in college halls, as a congenial visitor is to-day, and spending the afternoons, not the evenings, in discussions arising out of the conversation over the dinner-table. His ready wit and natural vivacity, his wide reading and serious purpose, made themselves felt. Even Colet the austere was delighted with him and begged him to stay. He was lecturing himself on St. Paul; let Erasmus take some part of the Old Testament and expound it to fascinated audiences. Oxford laid her spell upon the young Dutch canon—upon whom does she not?—but he was not yet ready. To give his life to sacred studies was the purpose that was riveting itself upon him; but he could not accomplish what he wished without Greek at the least—he never made any serious attempt to learn Hebrew—and Greek was not to be had in Oxford, hardly indeed anywhere in Western Europe outside Italy and perhaps Spain. Indeed, for some years to come this university was to display her characteristic, or may be her admirable, caution towards the new light offered to her from without.

We must bear in mind the well-reasoned hostility of the Church to—or at least hesitation about—the revival of learning. In the period we are considering the powers of evil were very real. Men instinctively accepted the existence of a kingdom of darkness, extending its borders over the sphere of knowledge as over the other sides of human activity. Greek was the language of some of the most licentious literature—Sappho's poems were burnt by the Church at Constantinople in 1073—and of many detestable heresies; and thus though the Council of Vienne, with missionary zeal, had recommended in 1311 that lectures in Greek—as in other languages of the heretical East—should be established in the universities of Paris, Bologna, Oxford, and Salamanca, the decree had not been carried out, and Greek was still regarded with suspicion by the orthodox. Their opposition dies with their lives, these guardians of the thing that is. Of the thing that cometh they know that 'if it be of God, they cannot overthrow it'. The silent flooding in of the main is to them more to be desired than the swift wave which in giving may destroy. Let us not think too lightly of them because they feared shadows which the light of time has dispelled. It needs no eyes to see where they were wrong: where they were right—and they were right often enough—can only be seen by taking trouble to inquire.

Of the condition of learning in England in the second half of the fifteenth century we do not yet know all that we might. Manuscripts that men bought or had written for them, books that they read, catalogues of libraries now scattered can tell us much, even though the owners are dead and speak not. Single facts, like cards for cardhouses, will not stand alone. There is still much to be done. Great libraries are only just beginning to gather up the manuscript minutiae which their books contain; to identify handwritings; to decipher monograms; to collect facts. But some day when the work has been done, we may well hope to be able to put bone to bone and breathe new life into them in a way which will make valuable contributions to our knowledge.

There is sometimes an inclination now to underestimate the effect of the Renaissance. The writers of that age were unsparingly contemptuous of their predecessors, and their verdict was for long accepted almost without question. The reaction against this has led to an undue extolling of the Middle Ages. It is true enough that many of the Schoolmen, though the humanists speak of them as hopelessly barbarous, were capable of writing Latin which, if not strictly classical, had yet an excellence of its own. But in view of the extracts given above from Ebrardus and John Garland it can hardly be maintained that there was much knowledge of Greek in Western Europe before the Renaissance. England was not ahead of France and Germany in the fifteenth century; and if Deventer school in 1475 was fed upon the monstrosities we have seen, it is not likely that Winchester and Eton had any better fare. Some sporadic examples there may have been of men who added a knowledge of the Greek character to their reminiscences of the *Graecismus*; just as at the present day it is not difficult to acquire a faint acquaintance with Oriental languages, enough to recognize the formation of words and plough out the letters, without any real knowledge. Colet and Fisher only began to learn Greek in their old age. One, the son of a Lord Mayor of London, made a name for himself as a lecturer at Oxford, and was advanced to be Dean of St. Paul's; the other, as head of a house at Cambridge and Chancellor of the University, promoted the foundation of the Lady Margaret's two colleges, Christ's and St. John's, which were to bring in the spirit of the Renaissance. It is impossible to suppose that men of such position would have spent the greater part of their lives without Greek, if there had been any facilities for them to learn it when they were young. Nor again would Erasmus, when teaching Greek at Cambridge in 1511, have chosen the grammars of Gaza and Chrysoloras to lecture upon, if his audience had been capable of anything better. Eminent scholars do not teach the elements at a university if boys are already learning them at school.

The condition of things may fairly be gauged by Duke Humfrey's collections for his library at Oxford. Of 130 books which he presented to the University in 1439, not one is Greek; of 135 given in 1443, only one—a vocabulary—is certainly Greek, four more are possibly, but not probably so. A little later in the century four Oxford men were pupils of Guarino in Ferrara; Grey († 1478) brought back manuscripts to Balliol and became Bishop of Ely; Gunthorpe († 1498) took his books with him to his deanery at Wells; but to only two of the four is any definite knowledge of Greek credited—Fleming († 1483), who compiled a Greek-Latin dictionary, and Free († 1465), who translated into Latin Synesius' treatise on baldness.

A discovery recently made by Dr. James of Cambridge has thrown unexpected light on the history of English scholarship at this period; and as it affords an example of the fruits to be yielded by careful research and synthesis, it may be detailed here. New Testament scholars have long been interested in a manuscript of the Gospels known, from its present habitation in the Leicester town-library, as the Leicester Codex; its date being variously assigned to the fourteenth or fifteenth century. In the handwriting there are some marked characteristics which make it easy to recognize; and in course of time other Greek manuscripts were discovered written by the same hand, two Psalters in Cambridge libraries, a Plato and Aristotle in the cathedral library at Durham, a Psalter and part of the lexicon of Suidas in Corpus at Oxford. But no clue was forthcoming as to their origin, until Dr. James found at Leiden a small Greek manuscript in the same hand, containing some letters of Aeschines and Plato, and a colophon stating that it had been written by Emmanuel of Constantinople for George Neville, Archbishop of York, and completed on 30 Dec. 1468. Where the various manuscripts were written and from what originals is not plain—the Suidas perhaps from a manuscript belonging at one time to Grosseteste; but the classical manuscripts were probably done for Neville in England during the prosperous years before his deportation to Calais in 1472, the Psalters and Gospels probably after that date at Cambridge; for the Paston Letters show that some of his disbanded household made their way to Cambridge, and Dr. Rendel Harris has ingeniously demonstrated that one Psalter and the Gospels were in fact at Cambridge with the Franciscans early in the sixteenth century. The presence of a Greek scribe in England about 1470 is an important fact.

Neville was released from prison through the intervention of Pope Sixtus IV, who about 1475 sent to England another Greek scribe and diplomatist, George Hermonymus of Sparta, charged with a letter to Edward IV. Besides Andronicus Contoblacas at Basle, Hermonymus was at the time the only Greek in Northern Europe who was prepared to teach his native tongue; in consequence most of the humanists of the day, Reuchlin, Erasmus, Budaeus and many others, turned to him for instruction, though he was indeed a poor teacher. He secured the Archbishop's release, and therewith a handsome reward to himself; but lingering on, he found himself compelled to spend about a year in London—in prison: some Italian merchants having trumped up against him a charge of espionage, from which he only escaped by paying the uttermost farthing. That he suffered such a disagreeable experience perhaps indicates that no one in London was much interested in him or his language.

Another Greek who was copying manuscripts in England at this time was John Serbopoulos, also of Constantinople, who between 1489 and 1500 wrote a number of Greek manuscripts at Reading: two copies of Gaza's Grammar, Isocrates *ad Demonicum* and *ad Nicoclem*, several commentators on Aristotle's Ethics, Chrysostom on St. Matthew, a Psalter and the completion of the Corpus Suidas which his fellow-countryman Emmanuel had begun. In one of his colophons (1494) he specifies Reading Abbey as his place of abode; for the others he merely says Reading. Possibly he was in the abbey the whole time; but even a temporary visit, during which he wrote Gaza and Isocrates, is an indication that one at least of the monastic houses was not hostile to the revival of learning.

Not that any doubt is possible on this point, since the researches of Abbot Gasquet into the life of William Selling, who was Prior of Christchurch, Canterbury, 1472–95. After entering the monastery, about 1448, Selling was sent to finish his studies at Canterbury College, the home of the Benedictines in Oxford.[1] In 1464 he was allowed to go with a companion, William Hadley, to Italy; where they spent two or three years over taking degrees in Theology, and heard lectures at Padua, Bologna, and Rome. Twice in later years Selling went to Italy again; and he brought back with him to England manuscripts of Homer and Euripides, and Livy, and Cicero's *de Republica*. Some of these have survived and are to be found in Cambridge libraries; others perished in the fire which broke out when Henry VIII's Visitors came to Canterbury to dissolve Christchurch. But Selling's interest in learning was not confined to the collection of manuscripts. A translation of a sermon of Chrysostom made by him in 1488 is extant; and an antiquarian visitor to Canterbury copied into his note-book 'certain Greek terminations, as taught by Dr. Sellinge of Christchurch'.

Another Churchman of this period who was interested in the revival of learning has recently been revealed to us by his books, John Shirwood, Bishop of Durham, 1483–93. He was an adherent of Neville whom we mentioned as the patron of Emmanuel of Constantinople; and having risen to prosperity as Neville rose, he did not desert his patron when Fortune's wheel went round. It does not appear that he was educated in Italy; but for a number

[1] The Canterbury gate of Christ Church, Oxford, still marks its site. A generation or so later Linacre and More were students there; both having a connexion with Canterbury.

of years he was in Rome, as a lawyer engaged in the Papal court; and to his good service there as King's proctor he probably owed his advancement to Durham. Whilst at Rome, he bought great numbers of the Latin classics, especially those which were coming fresh from the press of Sweynheym and Pannartz. Cicero seems to have held the first place in his affections, six volumes out of forty-two; the Orations, the Epistles, *de Finibus* and *de Oratore*, the two last being duplicated. History is well represented with Livy, Suetonius, Josephus, Plutarch, Polybius, and Dionysius of Halicarnassus; the last four in translations. In poetry he had Plautus and Terence, Horace, Martial, Juvenal, Seneca, and Statius; in archaeology Vitruvius and Frontinus; of the Fathers, Jerome, Lactantius, and the Confessions of Augustine.

Twice after becoming Bishop Shirwood went to Rome again, as ambassador; once in 1487 in company with Selling and Linacre: on the second occasion, in 1492–3, he died. His books, however, had already found their way home to Durham, where they were acquired by Foxe, Shirwood's successor in the see; and Foxe subsequently presented them to his newly-founded college of Corpus Christi in Oxford. It is interesting to contrast Shirwood's collection with books presented to the library of Durham monastery by John Auckland, who was Prior 1484–94. Not a single one of them is classical, not one printed; Aquinas, Bernard, Anselm, Grosseteste, Albertus Magnus, Chrysostom in Latin, Vincent de Beauvais, *Summa Bibliorum*, *Tractatus de scaccario moralis iuxta mores hominum, Exempla de ànimalibus.* The Prior's outlook was very different from the Bishop's.

Leland tells us that Shirwood had also a number of Greek books, which Tunstall found at Auckland in 1530; but only one of these has been traced, a copy of Gaza's Grammar written by John Rhosus of Crete in 1479, and bought by Shirwood at Rome. Where the rest are no one knows; doubtless scattered in many libraries, among people to whom the name of Shirwood has no meaning. One wonders why Foxe did not secure them for Corpus when he took the Latin books. He wanted Greek, but perhaps he considered the set of Aldus' Greek texts which he actually gave to Corpus, more worth having than Shirwood's manuscripts (for when Shirwood was collecting in Italy, the first book printed in Greek, the Florentine Homer, 1488, had not yet appeared): possibly he never saw them.

Time would fail us to tell of all the famous Englishmen who went to study in Italy in the last years of the fifteenth century, let alone those who went and did not win fame. Langton who became Bishop of Winchester, and, not content with Wykeham's foundation, started a school in his own palace at Wolvesey; Grocin, Linacre and William Latimer, who took part in Aldus' Greek Aristotle; Colet; Lily who went further afield, to Rhodes and Jerusalem; Tunstall and Stokesley and Pace—all these were Oxford men, and yet few of them returned to settle in Oxford and teach. Of their later lives much is known, though not so much as we could wish; but their connexion with this University cannot be precisely dated, because the university registers for just this period, 1471–1505, are missing. We cannot tell just when they graduated; and we miss the chance of contemporary notes added occasionally to names of distinction. We cannot even discover to what colleges they belonged.

In the last half of the fifteenth century there had been a beginning of Greek in Oxford. Thomas Chandler, Warden of New College, 1454–75, had some knowledge of it; and under his auspices an Italian adventurer of no merit, Cornelio Vitelli, came and taught here for a short time. For about two years, 1491–3, Grocin returned to lecture on Greek, as the result of his Italian studies. Colet was here about 1497–1505, until he became Dean of St. Paul's; but his lectures, as we have said, were on the Vulgate, not the Greek Testament. Of the rest that shadowy and fugitive scholar, William Latimer, was the only one of this band of Oxonians who definitely came back to live and work in the University; and he perhaps did not cast in his lot here until 1513. When he did return, he was not to be torn away again from his rooms at All Souls, under the shadow of St. Mary's tower. In 1516 More and Erasmus wished him to come and teach Greek to Fisher, Bishop of Rochester; but could not prevail with him. It would seem strange to-day for an Oxford scholar to be invited to become private tutor to the Chancellor of the sister University: he would probably shrink, as Latimer did, and find refuge in excuses. For eight or nine years, Latimer said, his studies had led him elsewhere, and he had not touched Latin and Greek. For the same reason he declared himself unable to help Erasmus in preparing for the second edition of his New Testament. What these studies were is nowhere told—Latimer's only printed work is two letters, one a mere note to Aldus, the other a long letter to Erasmus—but there is some reason to suppose that they were musical. He urged, too, that it was useless to hope the Bishop could make much progress in a month or two with such a language as Greek, over which Grocin had spent two years in Italy, and Linacre, Latimer, and Erasmus himself had laboured for many years: it would be much better to send to Italy for some one who could reside for a long time in the Bishop's household.

Though he remained faithful to Oxford, Latimer in his later years held two livings near Chipping Campden: in one, Weston-sub-Edge, he rebuilt his parsonage-house and left his initials W. L. in the stonework, in the other, Saintbury, there is a contemporary medallion of him in the East window, showing the tall, thin figure which George Lily describes.

At the time of Erasmus' first visit to England, 1499, London was far more a centre of the new intellectual life than either Oxford or Cambridge. He rejoiced in his first meeting with Colet, and in their walks in Oxford gardens in the soft October sunshine; his Prior at St. Mary's was benign and helpful; and he found a young compatriot, John

Sixtin, of Bolsward in East Friesland, studying law, and engaged with him in a contest of that arid elegance which the taste of the age still demanded. But in London he found Grocin at his City living, ready to lend him books, and perhaps already contemplating those lectures delivered two years later, on the Ecclesiastical Hierarchy of Dionysius, which brought him to such a surprising conclusion—a denial of the attribution of them to Dionysius the Areopagite, which in agreement with Colet he had set out to prove. In London was Linacre, just returned from Venice, full of Aldus' Greek Aristotle; to a supplementary volume of which he had sent a translation of Proclus' Sphere, a mathematical work then highly esteemed. He had been working on Aristotelian commentators, and was soon to lecture on the *Meteorologica*—a course which More, who was working for the Bar in London, attended. More himself not long afterwards lectured publicly in London on Augustine's *de Ciuitate Dei*, also a favourite work with the humanists. William Lily, returned from his pilgrimage, was at work perhaps already as a schoolmaster in London; and vying with More in translating the Greek Anthology into Latin elegiacs. Bernard Andreas, the blind poet of Toulouse, after trying his fortune in vain at Oxford, had insinuated himself into Henry VII's confidence, and was now attached to the court as tutor to Prince Arthur—an office from which Linacre attempted unsuccessfully to oust him—and busy with his history of the king's reign: a project which enjoyed royal favour, and was the forerunner of Polydore Vergil's creditable essay towards a critical history of England.

When Erasmus was again invited to England in 1505–6, the position had not changed. He writes to a friend in Holland: 'There are in London five or six men who are thorough masters of both Latin and Greek: even in Italy I doubt that you would find their equals. Without wishing to boast, it is a great pleasure to find that they think well of me.' To Colet in the following year, when he had said farewell, he writes from Paris: 'No place in the world has given me such friends as your City of London: so true, so learned, so generous, so distinguished, so unselfish, so numerous.' With the string of epithets we are not concerned: the point to remark is that it is of London he writes, not of either of the universities.

Under these circumstances, it is not surprising that Erasmus did not at once accept Colet's proposition in 1499 that he should stay and teach in Oxford. Whether provision was offered him or not, we do not know: he might perhaps have stayed on by right at St. Mary's, but he loved not the rule. We do know, however, that at Paris there certainly was no provision for him. In quest of Greek, in quest of the proper equipment for his life's work, he went back to the old precarious existence, pupils and starvation, the dependence and the flattery that he loathed. It is this last, indeed, that puts the sting into his correspondence with Batt. That loyal friend, ever coaxing money out of his complacent and generous patroness for dispatch to Paris, would now and then ask for a letter to her, to make the claims of the absent more vivid. At this Erasmus would boil over: 'Letters,' he writes, 'it 's always letters. You seem to think I am made of adamant: or perhaps that I have nothing else to do.' 'There is nothing I detest more than these sycophantic epistles.' Well he might; for this is the sort of thing he wrote.

You will remember that the Lady of Veere was named Anne of Borsselen. A letter of Erasmus to her begins: 'Three Annas were known to the ancients; the sister of Dido, whom the Muses of the Romans have consecrated to immortality; the wife of Elkanah, with whose praises Jewish records resound; and the mother of the Virgin, who is the object of Christian worship. Would that my poor talents might avail, that posterity may know of your piety and snow-white purity, and count you the fourth member of this glorious band! It was no mere chance that conferred upon you this name, making your likeness to them complete. Were they noble? So are you. Did they excel in piety? Yours, too, redounds to heaven. Were they steadfast in affliction? Alas that here, too, you are constrained to resemble them. Yet in my sorrow comfort comes from this thought, that God sends suffering to bring strength. Affliction it was that made the courage of Hercules, of Aeneas, of Ulysses shine forth, that proved the patience of Job.' This, of course, is only a brief epitome. After a great deal more in this strain, he concludes: 'I send you a poem to St. Anne and some prayers to address to the Virgin. She is ever ready to hear the prayers of virgins, and you I count not a widow, but a virgin. That when only a child you consented to marry, was mere deference to the bidding of your parents and the future of your race; and your wedded life was a model of patience. That now, when still no more than a girl, you repel so many suitors is further proof of your maiden heart. If, as I confidently presage, you persevere in this high course, I shall count you not amongst the virgins of Scripture innumerable, not amongst the eighty concubines of Solomon, but, with (I am sure) the approval of Jerome, among the fifty queens.'

The taste of that age liked the butter spread thick, and Erasmus' was the best butter. He relieved his mind the same day in a letter to Batt—which he did not shrink from publishing in the same volume with his effusion to the Lady Anne: 'It is now a year since the money was promised, and yet all you can say is, "I don't despair," "I will do my best." I have heard that from you so often that it quite makes me sick. The minx! She neglects her property to dally and flirt with her fine gentleman' (a young man whom Erasmus feared she would marry, as in fact she did, shortly afterwards). 'She has plenty of money to give to those scoundrels in hoods, but nothing for me, who can write books which will make her famous.' *In ira veritas.* But for Erasmus—and Batt—the rather simpering statue of Anne on the front of the town-hall at Veere would have little meaning for us to-day.

We must not judge Erasmus too hardly in his double tongue. Scholars of to-day, secure in their endowments, can hold their heads high; of their obligations to pious Founders no utterance is required save *coram Deo*—'vt nos his donis ad Tuam gloriam recte vtentes'. We hear much now of the artistic temperament which brooks no control, which at all costs must express its message to the world. No artist has ever burned with a fiercer fire than did Erasmus for the high tasks which his powers demanded of him; but at this period of his life there was no pious Founder to make his way plain. Later on, in all time of his wealth, he was generosity itself with his money, and inexorable in refusing honours and places that would have hindered him from his work.

V

ERASMUS' LIFE-WORK

IN August 1511 Erasmus returned to Cambridge. He was a different man from the young scholar who had determined twelve years before that it was no use for him to stay in Oxford. In the interval he had learnt what he wanted—Greek; he had had his desire and visited Italy; and now he came back to sit down to steady work, in accordance with his promise to Colet, in accordance with the purpose of his life, to advance the study of the Scriptures and the knowledge of God. It had been no light matter to learn Greek. Books were not abundant, and the only teacher to be had, Hermonymus of Sparta, was useless to him, neither could nor would impart the classical Greek that scholars wanted. So Erasmus was compelled to fall back on the best of all methods, to teach himself. He had no Liddell and Scott, no Stephanus; probably nothing better than a manuscript vocabulary copied from some earlier scholar, and amplified by himself. No wonder that he found Homer difficult and skipped over Lucian's long words. He exercised himself in translation, from Lucian, from Libanius, from Euripides. But that ready method of acquiring a new language—through the New Testament, was probably not open to him, for copies of the Gospels in Greek were rare, and not within the reach of a needy scholar's purse. However, he persevered, and at length he was satisfied. He never attained to Budaeus' mastery of Greek, but he had acquired a working knowledge which carried him as far as he wished to go.

His visit to Italy need not detain us long. Twenty-five years later he wrote to an Italian nobleman with whom he was engaged in controversy, to say that Italy had taught him nothing. 'When I came to Italy, I knew more Greek and Latin than I do now.' In the excitement of contention he perhaps 'remembered with advantages', for in Italy he had one great opportunity. He had published in 1500 at Paris a chrematistic work entitled *Collectanea Adagiorum,* a collection of Latin proverbs with brief explanations designed to be useful to the numerous public who aspired to write Latin with elegance. After the book was out, as authors do, he went on collecting, and on his way to Italy in 1506, he published a slightly enlarged edition, also in Paris. In Italy he made acquaintance with Aldus, and after finishing his year of superintendence over the pupils he had brought with him, he went, about the beginning of 1508, to dwell in the Neacademia at Venice. In September 1508 there appeared from Aldus' press a volume on the same subject, but very different in bulk; no longer *Collectanea Adagiorum,* but *Adagiorum Chiliades.* The Paris volume, a thin quarto, had contained about 800 proverbs, Aldus' had more than 3,000, and the commentary became so amplified, with occasional lengthy disquisitions on subjects moral and political, that nothing but a folio size would accommodate it.

Where this work was done, Erasmus does not specifically state. One passage gives the impression that he had made his new collections in England; but as one reason for his dissatisfaction with the first edition was the absence of citations from the Greek, it seems more probable that he really wrote the new book in Aldus' house at Venice. There, surrounded by the scholars of the New Academy, Egnatius, Carteromachus, Aleander, Urban of Belluno, besides Aldus himself and his father-in-law Asulanus, having at hand all the wealth of the Aldine Greek editions and the Greek manuscripts which were sent from far and near to be printed, Erasmus was thoroughly equipped to transform his quarto into folio, his hundreds into thousands. He tells us that the compositors printed as he wrote, and that he had hard work to keep pace with them. Some of his rough manuscripts—written rapidly in his smooth hand and flowing sentences—survive still to help us picture the scene. It is remarkable how little correction there is. Here and there a whole page is drawn straight through, to be rewritten, or a passage is inserted in the neat margin; but there is little botching, little mending of words or transposing of phrases, such as make the rough work of other humanists difficult reading. As he wished the sentences to run, so they flowed on to his pages, and so they actually were printed.

The importance of Erasmus' time in Italy is, then, that he completed, or at any rate published, the enlarged *Adagia*, his first considerable work, a book which carried his name far and wide throughout Europe, and won him fame amongst all who had pretensions to scholarship. No one reads it to-day. Except the composition of the schools, for which Erasmus is considered unclassical, there is little Latin writing now; but in its youth the book had a great vogue, and went through hundreds of reprints.

This second visit of Erasmus to Cambridge was under pleasant conditions. Fisher was interested in his work, and having been until recently President of Queens'—the foundation of Margaret of Anjou, which Elizabeth Woodville had succoured, York coming to the rescue of Lancaster—he was able without difficulty to secure rooms in college for his protégé. High up they are, at the head of a staircase, where undergraduates still cherish his name, and where his portrait—an heirloom from one generation to another—may be seen surrounded by prints of gentlemen in pink riding to hounds; quite a suitable collocation for this very humanly minded scholar. Besides his own work he lectured publicly for a few months. He began to teach Greek, and lectured on the grammar of Chrysoloras. Finding that this did not attract pupils, he changed to Gaza; which he evidently expected to be more popular. But he did not persevere. If his position was public (which is doubtful), there was no money to pay him for long; and it is a sign of the state of the University, that he found it no use to lecture on anything more advanced than grammar. The Schoolmen were still strongly entrenched.

Besides teaching Greek he also lectured on Jerome's Letters and his Apology against Ruffinus, books which, as we shall see, he was working at privately. He is said to have held for a time the professorship of Divinity founded in Cambridge, as in Oxford, in 1497 by the Lady Margaret, but the records are inadequate; and here too it is possible that his teaching was a private venture. He had no regular income except a pension from Lord Mountjoy, to which in 1512 Warham added the living of Aldington in Kent; and these were supplemented by occasional gifts from friends, which he courted by dedicating to them translations from Plutarch and Lucian, Chrysostom and Basil. But this was not enough. He was free in his tastes, and liked to be free in his spending. He needed a horse to ride, and a boy to attend upon him. In consequence we hear a good many complaints of penury, all through his three years at Cambridge, 1511 to 1514.

It is worth while to examine in detail the work that he completed during this period on the Letters of Jerome and the New Testament. One afternoon in Oxford in 1499 he had had a long discussion with Colet, and in the course of it had argued strongly against a point of view which Colet had derived from Jerome. Whether this set him on to read Jerome again—he was already quite familiar with him—is not clear; but a year later, when he was hard at work in Paris, he was already engaged upon correcting the text of Jerome, and adding a commentary, being specially interested in the Letters. So far did his admiration carry him that he writes to a friend, 'I am perhaps biased; but when I compare Cicero's style with Jerome's, I seem to feel something lacking in the prince of eloquence himself'. After he left Paris in 1501, we hear no more of Jerome till 1511. It may therefore fairly be argued that his early work was done on manuscripts found in Paris libraries, very likely those of the great abbeys of St. Victor or St. Germain-des-Prés.

Subsequently, in Cambridge, he again had access to manuscripts and completed his recension of the Letters. Robert Aldridge, a young Fellow of King's, afterwards Bishop of Carlisle, speaks of working with him at Jerome in Queens', probably helping him in collation. An early catalogue of the Queens' library does not contain any mention of Jerome, so that Erasmus had probably borrowed his manuscripts from elsewhere—perhaps, like those of the New Testament, from the Chapter Library at St. Paul's; for later on, when the book was in the press, he returned from Basle to England to consult the manuscripts again, and there is no reason to suppose that during his brief stay—not a full month —he went outside London. If this surmise were correct, the destruction of St. Paul's library in the fires of 1561 and 1666 would explain why so little has been discovered about the manuscripts which

Erasmus had for his Jerome. He himself, in his prefaces, gives little indication of them, beyond saying that they were very old and mutilated, and that some of them were written in Lombardic and Gothic characters. Perhaps some day a student of Jerome will arise who will be able to throw light on the matter from examination of the text at which Erasmus arrived.

To the New Testament—the other work which occupied his time at Cambridge—he had also turned his attention shortly after his return to Paris in 1500, beginning a commentary on the Epistles of St. Paul. At the first start he wrote four volumes of it, but then for some reason threw it aside, and never completed it, though his mind recurred to it at intervals; and on one occasion after a fall from his horse, in which he injured his spine, he vowed to St. Paul that he would finish it, if he recovered. Probably he felt that his vow was redeemed by his Paraphrases of the New Testament, which he wrote a few years later, beginning with St. Paul, and completing the Epistles before he undertook the Gospels.

His next work on the New Testament came to him at Louvain in 1504. Walking out one day to the Abbey of Parc, outside the town—a house of White Canons, Erasmus himself being a Black—he came upon a manuscript in their library, the Annotations of Valla on the New Testament. There was an affinity between his mind and that of the famous scholar-canon of St. John Lateran, who, in spite of his dependence on Papal patronage and favour, had been unable to keep his tongue from asking awkward questions, from inquiring even into the authenticity of the Donation of Constantine. Erasmus read the Annotations and liked their critical, scholarly tone, and the frequent citations of the original Greek. With the characteristic generosity of the age he was allowed to carry the manuscript away and print it in Paris, with a dedication to an Englishman, Christopher Fisher, perhaps a kinsman of the Bishop of Rochester.

From Paris he wrote to Colet to report progress, saying that he had learnt Greek and was ready to turn to the Scriptures, and asking him to interest English patrons in their common work. By this time Colet himself had become a patron, having been appointed Dean of St. Paul's. It is therefore not surprising to find that within a year Erasmus was established in London, living in a bishop's house, endowed by his old pupil Lord Mountjoy, and rejoicing in the society of the learned friends gathered in the capital. Chief among these was Colet, who lent him manuscripts from the Chapter Library of St. Paul's, and provided a copyist to write out the fruits of his labours, a one-eyed Brabantine, Peter Meghen by name, who acted also as Colet's private letter-carrier. Meghen wrote a bold, well-marked hand, which is easily recognizable, and in consequence his work has been traced in many libraries. The British Museum has a treatise of Chrysostom, translated by Selling, and written by

Meghen for Urswick, afterwards Dean of Windsor and Rector of Hackney, to present to Prior Goldstone of Canterbury. (Urswick was frequently sent on embassies, and had doubtless enjoyed the hospitality of Christchurch on his way between London and Dover.) At Wells there are a Psalter and a translation of Chrysostom on St. Matthew, which Urswick, as executor to Sir John Huddelston, knight, caused Meghen to write in 1514 for presentation to the Cistercians of Hailes, in Gloucestershire. The Bodleian has a treatise written by him in 1528 for Nicholas Kratzer to present to Henry VIII; and Wolsey's Lectionary at Christ Church, Oxford, is probably in Meghen's hand.

But what concern us here are some manuscripts in the British Museum and the University Library at Cambridge, written by Meghen in 1506 and 1509 at Colet's order for presentation to his father, Sir Henry Colet, Lord Mayor of London, and containing in parallel columns the Vulgate and another Latin translation of the New Testament, 'per D. Erasmum Roterodamum'. Part and possibly all of this work was done by Erasmus, therefore, during this second residence in England in 1505–6. He tells us that he received two Latin manuscripts from Colet, which he found exceedingly difficult to decipher; but one cannot make a new translation from the Latin. To the Greek manuscripts used on this occasion he gives no clue.

In connexion with this help and encouragement shown by Colet as Dean to a foreign scholar, it is worth while to mention the visit to London in 1509 of Cornelius Agrippa, the famous philosopher and scientist, who had been sent to England by Maximilian on a diplomatic errand, which he describes as 'a very secret business'. During his stay, which lasted into 1510, he tells us that 'I laboured much over the Epistles of St. Paul, in the company of John Colet, a man most learned in Catholic doctrine, and of the purest life; and from him I learnt many things that I did not know'. Erasmus was in England at the time of this visit of Agrippa; but unfortunately he makes no allusion to it, neither in his life of Colet, nor in his later correspondence with Agrippa, nor, so far as I know, elsewhere in his works. If he had done so, it might have solved a problem which is very curious in the case of a public man of his fame and position, and of whom so much is otherwise known. From the autumn of 1509, when he returned from Italy and wrote the Praise of Folly in More's house in Bucklersbury, until April 1511, when he went to Paris to print it, Erasmus completely disappears from view. He published nothing, no letter that he wrote survives, we have no clue to his movements. If it had been any one else, we might almost conjecture that, like Hermonymus, he was in prison. It was just during this period that Cornelius Agrippa was in London. If either had mentioned the other, we should have a spark to illumine this singular belt of darkness.

When Erasmus returned to Cambridge in 1511,

he was already familiar with the field in which he was going to work; but the precise order in which his scheme unfolded itself, whether the Greek text was his first aim or an afterthought, is not clear, his utterances being perhaps intentionally ambiguous. During these three years in Cambridge he refers occasionally to the 'collation' and 'castigation' of the New Testament, so that evidently he was engaged with the four Greek manuscripts, which, according to an introduction in his first edition, he had before him for his first recension. One of these has been identified, the Leicester Codex written by Emmanuel of Constantinople, which, as already mentioned, was with the Franciscans at Cambridge early in the sixteenth century.

By 1514 he was ready. In the last three years he had completed Jerome and the New Testament, and had also prepared for the press some of Seneca's philosophical writings, from manuscripts at King's and Peterhouse; besides lesser pieces of work. A difficulty arose about the printing. In 1512 he had been in negotiation with Badius Ascensius of Paris to undertake Jerome and a new edition of the *Adagia*. What actually happened is not known. But in December 1513 he writes to an intimate friend that he has been badly treated about the *Adagia* by an agent—a travelling bookseller, who acted as go-between for printers and authors and public; that instead of taking them to Badius and offering him the refusal, the knavish fellow had gone straight to Basle and sold them, with some other work of Erasmus, to a printer who had only just completed an edition of the *Adagia.* Erasmus' indignation does not ring true. It is highly probable that he was in search of a printer with greater resources than Badius, who as yet had produced nothing of any importance in Greek, and would therefore be unable to do justice to the New Testament; and that accordingly he had commissioned the agent to negotiate with a firm which by now had established a great reputation—that of Amorbach and Froben, in Basle. His attention had perhaps been aroused by a flattering mention of him in a preface written in Froben's name for the pirated edition of the *Adagia,* August 1513, to which Erasmus was referring in the letter just quoted. Rumour had spread through Europe that Erasmus was dead—it was repeated six months later in a book printed at Vienna—and the Basle circle deplored the loss that this would mean to learning.

There were other reasons for this choice, apart from the excellence of the printers. Erasmus had never been happy in Paris. He had often been ill beside the sluggish Seine, and had only found his health again by leaving it. The theologians were still predominant there, and Louis XII had a way of interfering with scholars who discovered any freedom of thought. Standonck, for instance, the refounder of Montaigu, had had to disappear in 1499–1500. For Erasmus to sit in Paris for two or three years while his books were being printed, would have been at least a penance. But Basle was very different. The Rhine, dashing against the piers of the bridge which joined the Great and Little towns, brought fresh air and coolness and health. The University, founded in 1460, was active and liberally minded. The town had recently (1501) thrown in its lot with the confederacy of Swiss cantons, thereby strengthening the political immunity which it had long enjoyed. Between the citizens and the religious orders complete concord prevailed; and finally, except Paris, there was no town North of the Alps which could vie with Basle in the splendour and number of the books which it produced. This is how a contemporary scholar[1] writes of the city of his adoption. 'Basle to-day is a residence for a king. The streets are clean, the houses uniform and pleasant, some of them even magnificent, with spacious courts and gay gardens and many delightful prospects; on to the grounds and trees beside St. Peter's, over the Dominicans', or down to the Rhine. There is nothing to offend the taste even of those who have been in Italy, except perhaps the use of stoves instead of fires, and the dirt of the inns, which is universal throughout Germany. The climate is singularly mild and agreeable, and the citizens polite. A bridge joins the two towns, and the situation on the river is splendid. Truly Basle is *βασίλεια*, a queen of cities.'

In 1513 the two greatest printers of Basle were in partnership, John Amorbach and John Froben. Amorbach, a native of the town of that name in

[1] Beatus Rhenanus, *Res Germanicae*, 1531, pp. 140, 1.

Franconia, had taken his M.A. in Paris, and then had worked for a time in Koberger's press at Nuremberg. About 1475 he began to print at Basle, and for nearly forty years devoted all his energies to producing books that would promote good learning; being, however, far too good a man of business to be indifferent to profit. His ambition was to publish worthily the four Doctors of the Church. Ambrose appeared in 1492, Augustine in 1506, and Jerome succeeded. The work was divided amongst many scholars. Reuchlin helped with the Hebrew and Greek, and spent two months in Amorbach's house in the summer of 1510 to bring matters forward. Subsequently his province fell to Pellican, the Franciscan Hebraist, and John Cono, a learned Dominican of Nuremberg, who had mastered Greek at Venice and Padua, and had recently returned from Italy with a store of Greek manuscripts copied from the library of Musurus. Others who took part in the work were Conrad Leontorius from the Engental; Sapidus, afterwards head master of the Latin school at Schlettstadt; and Gregory Reisch, the learned Prior of the Carthusians at Freiburg, who seems to have been specially occupied with Jerome's Letters.

Amorbach's sons, Bruno, Basil, and Boniface, were just growing up to take their father's place, when he died on Christmas Day, 1513. The eldest, Bruno, was born in 1485, and easily paired off with Basil, who was a few years younger. They went to school together at Schlettstadt, under Crato

Hofman, in 1497. In 1500 they matriculated at Basle; in 1501 they went to Paris, where in 1504–5 they became B.A., and in 1506 M.A. Bruno was enthusiastic for classical studies, and enjoyed life in Paris, where he certainly had better opportunities, especially of learning Greek, than he had at Basle; so his father allowed him to stay on. Basil was destined for the law, and was sent to work under Zasius at Freiburg. The youngest son, Boniface, 1495–1562, also went to school at Schlettstadt; but when his time came for the university, his father preferred to keep him at home under his own eye. He was rather dissatisfied with Bruno, who as a Paris graduate had begun to play the fine gentleman, and was spending his money handsomely, as other young men have been known to do. The vigorous, straightforward old printer had made the money himself by steady hard work, and he had no intention of letting his son take life too easily. So he wrote him a piece of his mind, in fine, forcible Latin.

JOHN AMORBACH TO HIS ELDEST SON, BRUNO, IN PARIS: from Basle, 23 July 1507.

'I cannot imagine, Bruno, what you do, to spend so much money.[1] You took with you 7 crowns; and supposing that you spent 2, or at the outside 3, on your journey, you must have had 4 left—unless perhaps you paid for your companion, which I did not tell you to do. Very likely his father has more

[1] Bruno, satis admirari non possum quid agas vt tot pecunias consumas.

money than I have, but does not give it to him; no more do I give you money to pay for other people. It is quite enough for me to support you and your brothers, indeed more than enough.

Then, directly you reached Paris, you received 12 crowns from John Watensne. Also you had 9 for your horse, as you say in your letter. Also 9 more from John Watensne, which I paid to Wolfgang Lachner at the Easter fair at Frankfort; also 15 at midsummer. Add these together and you will see that you have had 52 crowns in 9 months.

Perhaps you imagine that money comes to me anyhow. You know that for the last two years I have not been printing. We are living upon capital, the whole lot of us.[1] I have to provide for my household.[2] I have to provide for your brother Basil, and for Boniface, whom I have sent to Schlettstadt. I ought, too, to do something for your sister: for several sober and honourable men are at me about her, and I do not like to be unfair towards her. So just remember that you are not the only one.

You may take it for sure that I cannot, and will not, give you more than 22 or 23 crowns a year, or at the most 24. If you can live on that at Paris, well: I will undertake to let you have it for some years. But if it is not enough, come home and I will feed you at my table. Think it over and let me know by the next messenger: or else come yourself.

I have been told on good authority that in the

[1] Consumimus omnes de capitali.

[2] Habeo prouidere domui meae.

town ⟨lodgings, as opposed to a college⟩ one can live quite decently on 16 or at most 20 crowns: also that sometimes three or four students, or more, take a house or a room, and then club together and engage a cook, and that their weekly bills scarcely amount to a teston ⟨$\frac{1}{5}$ of a crown⟩ a head. If that is so, join a party like that and live carefully.

Good-bye. Your mother sends her love.

Your affectionate father,

John Amorbach.

No answer came back, and on 18 August John Amorbach wrote again. Think of a modern parent waiting a month for an answer to such a communication and getting none! It might quite well have come. But posts were slow and uncertain; and when he wrote again, the father's righteous indignation had somewhat abated. It was not till 16 October that Bruno replied, but with a very proper letter. He was a good fellow, and knew what he owed to his father. After expressing his regrets and determination to live within his allowance in future, he goes on: 'There is a man just come from Italy, who is lecturing publicly on Greek. ⟨This was Francis Tissard of Amboise, who began lecturing on Lascaris' Greek Grammar.⟩ I have so long been wishing to learn this language, and here at length is an opportunity. I have plunged headlong into it, and with such a teacher I feel sure of satisfying my desires, which are as eager as any inclinations of the senses. So please allow me to stay a few months longer, and then

I shall be able to bring home some Greek with me. After that I will come whenever you bid me.' Next summer he did return and settled down to work in the press. It was well worth while, even for a scholar who was eager to go on learning, and was inclined to grudge time given to business: for with Jerome beginning and all the scholars whom we mentioned coming in and out, Amorbach's house in Klein-Basel became an 'Academy' which could bear comparison with Aldus' at Venice. It was worth Boniface's while, too, to take his course at Basle under such circumstances; especially as in 1511 John Cono began to teach Greek and Hebrew regularly to the printer's sons and to any one else who wished to come and learn. It is worth noticing that not one of these young men went to Italy for his humanistic education.

Amorbach's partner, John Froben, 1460–1527, was a man after his own heart: open and easy to deal with, but of dogged determination and with great capacity for work. He was not a scholar. It is not known whether he ever went to a University, and it is doubtful whether he knew any Latin; certainly the numerous prefaces which appear in his books under his name are not his own, but came from the pens of other members of his circle. So the division came naturally, that Amorbach organized the work and prepared manuscripts for the press, while Froben had the printing under his charge. In later years, after Amorbach's death, the marked advance in the output of the firm as regards type and paper and title-pages and designs may be attributed to Froben, who was man of business enough to realize the importance of getting good men to serve him—Erasmus to edit books, Gerbell and Oecolampadius to correct the proofs, Graf and Holbein to provide the ornaments. For thirteen years he was Erasmus' printer-in-chief, and produced edition after edition of his works, both small and great; and whilst he lived, he had the call of almost everything that Erasmus wrote. It is quite exceptional to find any book of Erasmus published for the first time elsewhere during these years 1514–27. A few were given to Martens at Louvain, mostly during Erasmus' residence there, 1517–21, one or two to Schurer at Strasburg, one or two more to a Cologne printer; but for one of these there is evidence to show that Froben had declined it, because his presses were too busy. It is pleasant to find that the harmony of this long co-operation was never disturbed. Erasmus occasionally lets fall a word of disapproval; but what friends have ever seen eye to eye in all matters?

When Froben died in October 1527 as the result of a fall from an upper window, Erasmus wrote with most heartfelt sorrow a eulogy of his friend. 'He was the soul of honesty himself, and slow to think evil of others; so that he was often taken in. Of envy and jealousy he knew as little as the blind do of colour. He was swift to forgive and to forget even serious injuries. To me he was most generous, ever seeking excuses to make me presents. If I ordered my servants to buy anything, such as a piece of cloth for a new coat, he would get hold of the bill and pay it off; and he would accept nothing himself, so that it was only by similar artifices that I could make him any return. He was enthusiastic for good learning, and felt his work to be his own reward. It was delightful to see him with the first pages of some new book in his hands, some author of whom he approved. His face was radiant with pleasure, and you might have supposed that he had already received a large return of profit. The excellence of his work would bear comparison with that of the best printers of Venice and Rome. Six years before his death he slipped down a flight of steps on to a brickwork floor, and injured himself so severely that he never properly recovered: but he always pretended that the effects had passed away. Last year he was seized with a serious pain in his right ankle, and the doctors could do nothing except to suggest that the foot should be taken off. Some alleviation was brought by the skill of a foreign physician, but there was still a great deal of pain in the toes. However, he was not to be deterred from making the usual journeys to Frankfort ⟨in March and September for the book-fairs⟩ and rode on horseback both ways. We entreated him to take more care of himself, to wear more clothes when it was cold; but he could not be induced to give in to old age, and abandon the habits of a vigorous lifetime. All lovers of good learning will unite to lament his loss.'

If Erasmus was fortunate in his printer, he was

still more fortunate in the friend and confidant whom he found awaiting him at Basle, Beat Bild of Rheinau, 1485–1547, known then and now as Beatus Rhenanus, one of the choicest spirits of his own or any age. His father was a butcher of Rheinau who left his home because of continued ravages by the Rhine which threatened to sweep away the town. Settling in Schlettstadt, a free city of the Empire near by, he rose to the highest civic offices, and sent his son to the Latin school under first Crato Hofman and then Gebwiler. Beatus was contemporary there with Bruno and Basil Amorbach, and staying on longer than they did, rose to be a 'praefect' in the school, which a few years later, according to Thomas Platter, had 900 boys in it. This number seems large for a town of perhaps not more than four or five thousand inhabitants; but it was equalled by the school at Alcmar in the days of Bartholomew of Cologne, and by Deventer, as we have seen, it was far surpassed. In 1503 Beatus went to Paris, and there overtook the Amorbach boys who had two years' start of him; becoming B.A. in 1504 and M.A. in 1505, a year before Bruno. After his degree he stayed on in Paris as corrector to the press of Henry Stephanus for two years; and then returning home engaged himself in a similar capacity to Schurer at Strasburg, also giving a hand with editions of new texts. In 1511, attracted by the fame of the good Dominican, John Cono, he went to Basle to work for the elder Amorbach and take lessons under Cono with the sons. When Erasmus came, Beatus at once fell under his spell, and subordinated his own projects to the requirements of his friend's more important undertakings.

That indeed is Beatus' great characteristic throughout his life. He was well off, for his father 'by the blessing of God on his ingenious endeavour had arisen to an ample estate'; and thus the son was not obliged to seek reward. He gave himself, therefore, unstintingly to any work that needed doing for his friends, editing, correcting, supervising; and usually suppressing the part he had taken in it. His own achievements are nevertheless considerable. The bibliographers have discovered sixty-eight books in which he had a capital share; and though a large number of these appear to be mere reprints of books printed in France or Italy—the law of copyright in those days was, as might be expected, uncertain—, there is a residue in which he really did original work: some notes on the history and geography of Germany which he composed, and editions of Pliny's Natural History, Tacitus, Tertullian and Velleius Paterculus—the latter having an almost romantic interest from the fortunes of the manuscript on which it is based. A measure of the confidence which Erasmus subsequently reposed in both his judgement and his good faith is that in 1519 and 1521, when he had decided to publish some more of his letters, he just sent to Beatus bundles of the rough drafts he had preserved, and told him to select and edit them at his discretion.

A sketch of Beatus, written at his death by

John Sturm of Strasburg, the friend of Ascham, gives a picture of the life he led at Schlettstadt during his last twenty years: the plain, simple living in the great house inherited from his father, without luxury or display, attended upon by an old maidservant and a young servant-pupil, given to friends but not allowing hospitality to infringe upon his work, lapped in such quiet as to seem almost solitude; the daily round being dinner at ten, in the afternoon a walk in his gardens outside the city walls, and supper at six. Gentle and accommodating, modest and diffident in spite of his learning, reluctant to talk of himself, and slow to take offence —it is no wonder that he held the affections of his friends. Well might Erasmus liken him to the blessed man of the first Psalm, 'who shall be as a tree planted by the waterside.'

We have seen Beatus' enthusiasm for queenly Basle. Of his native town he was not so proud; though it has good Romanesque work in St. Fides' church and rich Gothic in the minster, and though Wimpfeling had just built a beautiful Renaissance house with Italian designs round its bay window and medallions of Roman Emperors on the pilasters. The school, too, was famous throughout Germany; and Lazarus Schurer had started a creditable printing-press. Yet to Beatus the minster is only 'rather good, but modern', the Dominicans' house 'mediocre', the nuns' buildings 'unhealthy', the people 'simple and resourceless, as you would expect with vine-growers, and too fond of drinking'.

'There is nothing remarkable here', he says, 'but the fortifications; indeed we are a stronghold rather than a city. The walls are circular, built of elegant brick and with towers of some pretensions.' What pleased him as much as anything was that the ramparts were covered in for almost the whole of their length, and thus afforded protection to the night-guards against what he calls 'celestial injuries'.

One reason that we know Beatus so well is that his library has survived almost intact, as well as a great number of letters which he received. At his death he left his books to the town of Schlettstadt; and there they still are, forming the major and by far the most important part of the town library. It is a wonderful collection of about a thousand volumes, some of them extremely rare; many bought by him in his Paris days, some presents from friends sent or brought from far with dedicatory inscriptions. Hardly a book has not his name and the date when he acquired it, or other marks of his use. But they have not yet come to their full usefulness, for there is no adequate catalogue of them. In many cases their direct value has passed away. No one wishes to read the classics or the Fathers in the texts current in the sixteenth century; yet behind printed books lie manuscripts, and from examination of manuscripts on which printed texts are based, we can gather many useful indications to throw light on the tradition of the classics, the gradual steps by which the past has come down to us.

Besides such texts there are multitudes of original compositions of Beatus' own period, books of great value for the history of scholarship; many of them requiring to be dated with more precision than is attainable on the surface. It will be a signal service to learning when a trained bibliographer takes Beatus Rhenanus' books in hand and gives us a scientific catalogue.

These were some of the friends who were in Basle when Erasmus first began to think of sending his work there to be printed. By the summer of 1514 the preliminary negotiations had been satisfactorily concluded and he set out. The story which he tells of his arrival is well known. Amorbach was now dead; so he marched into the printing-house and asked for Froben. 'I handed him a letter from Erasmus, saying that I was a familiar friend of his, and that he had charged me to arrange for the publication of his works; that any undertaking I made would be as valid as if made by him: finally, that I was so like Erasmus that to see me was to see him. He laughed and saw through the joke. His father-in-law, old Lachner, paid my bill at the inn, and carried me off, horse and baggage to his house.'

He was not at first sure whether he would stay: he might get the work better done at Venice or at Rome. But the attractions of the printer's house and circle were not to be resisted; and gradually, one after another, the books which he had brought were undertaken by Froben, a new edition of the *Adagia*, Seneca, the New Testament, Jerome. The way in which the printing was carried out illustrates the critical standards of the age. Erasmus was absent from Basle during the greater part of the time when Seneca was coming through the press; and the proofs were corrected by Beatus Rhenanus and a young man named Nesen. Under such circumstances a modern author would feel that he had only himself to thank for any defects in the book. Not so Erasmus. He boils over with annoyance against the correctors for the blunders they let pass. The idea that so magnificent a person as an editor or author should correct proofs had not arisen. It was the business of the young men who had been hired to do this drudgery; and all blame rested with them. So far as the evidence goes, it was the same all through Erasmus' life. In the case of one of his most virulent apologies (1520) he says that he corrected all the proofs himself; but from the stress he lays on the loss of time involved, it is clear that he regarded this as something exceptional, and not to be repeated. With the *Adagia* published by Aldus (1508) he says that he cast his eye over the final proofs, not in search of errors, but to see whether he wished to make any changes. But in the main his books, like everybody else's, were left to the care of others.

The fact is that in the splendour of the new invention of printing, the possibilities of accompanying error had not been realized. In just the same spirit the idea went abroad that when a book had been printed, its manuscript original had no value. We have seen how Erasmus was allowed to carry off the manuscript of Valla from Louvain to Paris. Aldus received codices from all parts of Europe, sent by owners with the request that they should be printed; but no desire for their return. In 1531 Simon Grynaeus came from Basle to Oxford and was given precious texts from college libraries to take back with him and have published. Generosity helped to mislead. To keep a manuscript to oneself for personal enjoyment seemed churlish. If it were printed, any one who wished might enjoy it. That any degeneration might come in by the way, that the printed text might contain blunders, was not perceived. The process seemed so straightforward, so mechanical; as certain a method of reproduction as photography. But the human element in it was overlooked. *Humanum est errare.*

It was the same with the New Testament as with Seneca. When the form of the work had been decided upon—a Greek text side by side with Erasmus' translation, and notes at the end—two young scholars, Gerbell and Oecolampadius, were installed in charge of the book. For the Greek Erasmus had expected, he tells us, to find at Basle some manuscript which he could give to the printers without further trouble. But he was annoyed to find that there was none available which was good enough, and he positively had to go through the one that he selected from beginning to end before he could entrust it to his correctors. In addition to this he put into their hands another manuscript, which had been borrowed from Reuchlin; presumably to help them in case they should have any difficulty in deciphering the first. However, after a time he discovered that they were taking liberties, and following the text of the second manuscript, wherever they preferred its reading: as though the editing were in their own hands. He took it from them and found another manuscript which agreed more closely with the first. For the book of Revelation only one Greek manuscript was available; and at the end five verses and a bit were lacking through the loss of a leaf. Erasmus calmly translated them back from the Latin, but had the grace to warn the reader of the fact in his notes.

As to the translation, an interesting point is that it is modified considerably from the translation which he had made in 1505–6, and is brought closer to the text of the Vulgate. In the second edition of the New Testament, March 1519, he explains in a preliminary apology that he had changed back in this way in 1516 from fear lest too great divergence from the Vulgate might give offence. But the book was on the whole so well received that he soon realized that the time was ripe for more advanced scholarship. His earlier version was the best that he could do, in simplicity of style and fidelity to the original. Accordingly in 1519 he introduced it with the most minute care, even such trivial variations as *ac* or *-que* for *et* being restored. The transformation was not without its effects. Numerous passages were objected to by the orthodox; as for example, when he translates λόγος in the first verse of St. John's Gospel by *sermo,* instead of *verbum,* as in the Vulgate and the edition of 1516.

The New Testament appeared in March 1516, dedicated by permission to the Pope; in the following autumn came Jerome, in nine volumes, of which four were by Erasmus, dedicated to the Archbishop of Canterbury: and thus the Head of the Church and one of his most exalted suffragans lent their sanction to an advancement of learning which theological faculties in the universities viewed with the gravest suspicion.

Erasmus had now reached his highest point. He had equipped himself thoroughly for the work he desired to do. He was the acknowledged leader of a large band of scholars, who looked to him for guidance and were eagerly ready to second his efforts; and with the resources of Froben's press at his disposal, nothing seemed beyond his powers and his hopes. Wherever his books spread, his name was honoured, almost reverenced. Material honours and wealth flowed in upon him; and he was continually receiving enthusiastic homage from strangers. He saw knowledge growing from more to more, and bringing with it reform of the Church and that steady betterment of the evils of the world which wise men in every age desire. In all this his part was to be that of a leader: not the only one, but in the front rank. He enjoyed his position, feeling that he was fitted for it; but he was not puffed up. In his dreams of what he would do with his life, he had ever seen himself advancing not the name of Erasmus but the glory of God. In his later years he became impatient of criticism, and resented with great bitterness even difference of opinion, unless expressed with the utmost caution; to hostile critics his language is often quite intolerable. But the spirit underlying this is not mere vanity. No doubt it wounded him to be evil spoken of, to have his pre-eminence called in question, to be shown to have made mistakes: but the real ground of his resentment was rather vexation that anything should arise to mar the unanimity of the humanist advance toward wider knowledge. Conscious of singleness of purpose, it was a profound disappointment to him to have his sincerity doubted, to be treated as an enemy by men who should have been his friends.

Into the discord of the years that followed I do not propose to enter. They were years of disappointment to Erasmus; disappointment that grew ever deeper, as he saw the steady growth of reform broken by the sudden shocks of the Reformation and barred by subsequent reaction. Throughout it all he never lost his faith in the spread of knowledge, and gave his energies consistently to help this great cause. He produced more editions of the Fathers, either wholly or in part: Cyprian, Arnobius, Hilary, Jerome again, Chrysostom, Irenaeus, Athanasius, Ambrose, Augustine, Lactantius, Alger, Basil, Haymo, and Origen; the last named in the concluding months of his life. The storms that beat round him could not stir him from his principles. To neither reformer nor reactionary would he concede one jot, and in consequence from each side he was vilified. He was drawn into a series of deplorable controversies, which estranged him from many; but of his real friends he lost not one. It is pleasant to see the devotion with which Beatus Rhenanus and Boniface Amerbach comforted his last years; never wavering in the service to which they had plighted themselves in the enthusiasm of youth.

The chance survival of the following note enables us to stand by Erasmus' bedside in his last hours. It was written by one of the Frobens, possibly his godson and namesake, Erasmius, to Boniface Amerbach, and it may be dated early in July 1536, perhaps on the 11th, the last sunset that Erasmus was to see. 'I have just visited the Master, but without his knowing. He seems to me to fail very much: for his tongue cleaves to his palate, so that you can scarcely understand him when he speaks. He is drawing his breath so deep and quick, that I cannot but wonder whether he will live through the night. So far he has taken nothing to-day except some chicken-broth. I have sent for Sebastian ⟨Munster, the Hebraist⟩. If he comes, I will have him introduced into the room, but without the Master's knowledge, in order that he may hear what I have heard. I am sending you this word, so that you may come quickly.'

Erasmus' last words were in his own Dutch speech: 'Liever Got'.

No account of Erasmus must omit to tell how he laboured for peace. Well he might. In his youth he had seen his native Holland torn between the Hoeks and the Cabeljaus, the Duke of Gueldres and the Bishop of Utrecht, with occasional intervention by higher powers. Year after year the war had dragged on, with no decisive settlement, no relief to the poor. One of his friends, Cornelius Gerard, wrote a prose narrative of it; another, William Herman, composed a poem of Holland weeping for her children and would not be comforted. *Dulce bellum inexpertis.* War sometimes seems purifying and ennobling to those whose own lives have never been jeoparded, who have never seen men die: but not so to those who have known and suffered. Throughout his life Erasmus never wearied of ensuing peace; and for its sake he reproved even kings. In 1504 he was allowed to deliver a panegyric of congratulation before the Archduke Philip the Fair, who had just returned from Spain to the Netherlands; and after sketching a picture of a model prince, inculcated upon him the duty of maintaining peace. In 1514 he wrote to one of his patrons, brother of the Bishop of Cambray, a letter on the wickedness of war, obviously designed for publication and actually translated into German by an admirer a few years later, to give it wider circulation. In 1515 the enlarged *Adagia* contained an essay on the same theme, under the title quoted above: words which, translated into English, were again and again reprinted during the nineteenth century by Peace Associations and the Society of Friends. In 1516 he was appointed Councillor to

Philip's son, Charles, who at 16 had just succeeded to the crowns of Spain. His first offering to his young sovereign was counsel on the training of a Christian prince, with due emphasis on his obligations for peace. In 1517 he greeted the new Bishop of Utrecht, Philip of Burgundy, with a 'Complaint of Peace cast forth from all lands', *Querela Pacis vndique profligatae.* And besides these direct invocations, in his other writings, his pen frequently returns upon the same high argument. For a brief period in his life it seemed as though peace might come back. Maximilian's death in 1519 followed by Charles' election to the Empire placed the sovereignty of Western and Central Europe in the hands of three young men, who were chivalrous and impressionable, Henry and Francis and Charles: only the year before they had been treating for universal peace. If they would really act in concord, it seemed as though the Golden Age might return, and Christendom show a united face against the watchful and unwearying Turk. But though the sky was clear, the weather was what Oxfordshire folk call foxy. Strife of nations, strife of creeds cannot in a moment be allayed. Suddenly the little clouds upon the horizon swelled up and covered the heaven with the darkness of night; and before the dawn broke into new hope, Erasmus had laid down his pen for ever, and was at rest from his service to the Prince of Peace.

VI

FORCE AND FRAUD

As you stand on the Piazza dei Signori at Verona, at one side rises the massive red-brick tower of the Scaliger palace, lofty, castellated at its top, with here and there a small window, deep set in the old masonry, and the light that is allowed to pass inwards, grudgingly crossed by bars of rusty iron —a place of defence and perhaps of tyranny, within which life is secure indeed, but grim and sombre. Opposite, in an angle of the square, stands a very different building, the Palazzo del Consiglio. It has only two storeys, but each of these is high and airy; above is a fine chamber, through whose ample windows streams in the sun; below is a pleasant loggia, supported by slender columns. Marble cornices and balustrades give a sense of richness, and the wall-spaces are bright with painting and ornament. The spacious galleries invite to enjoyment, to pace their length in free light-hearted talk, or to stand and watch the life moving below, with the sense of gay predominance that the advantage of height confers.

The two buildings typify most aptly the ages to which they belong: the contrast between them is as the gulf between the Middle Ages and the Renaissance. Step back in thought to the twelfth century, and we find civilization struggling for its very existence. Few careers were possible. Above all was the soldier, ruthlessly spreading murder and desolation, and expecting no mercy when his own turn came; in the middle were the merchant and the craftsman, relying on strong city walls and union with their fellows, and the lawyer building up a system, and profiting when men fell out; underneath was the peasant, pitiably dependent on others. On all sides was bestial cruelty and reckless ignorance: the overmastering care of life to find shelter and protection. How strong, how luxuriously strong seemed that tower, with so few apertures to admit the enemy and the pursuer! once inside, who would wish to stir abroad? For the man who would think or study there was only one way of life, to become sacrosanct in the direct service of God. The Church, with splendid ideals before it, was exerting itself to crush barbarism, and its forts were garrisoned by men of spirit, whose courage was not that of the destroyer. In the monasteries, if anywhere, was to be found that peace which the world cannot give, the life of contemplation, in which can be felt the hunger and thirst after knowledge.

By the middle of the sixteenth century the scene has changed. Much blood has flowed through the arches of time; and now the conqueror has learnt from the Church to be merciful, from nascent science to be strong. He can spread peace wherever his sword reaches; and fear that of old ruled all under the sun, now can walk only in dark places. Walls no longer bring comfort, and soon they are to be thrown down to make way for the broad streets which will carry the movement outwards; and, most significant change, the country house with 'its gardens and its gallant walks' takes the place of the grange. From the thraldom of terror what an escape, to light, air, freedom, activity! The gates of joy are opened, the private citizen learns to live, to follow choice not necessity, to give the reins to his spirit and take hold on the gifts that Nature spreads before him.

In the pursuit of peace, human progress has lain in the enlargement of the units of government capable of holding together; from villages to towns, from towns to provinces, from provinces to nations. The last step had been the achievement of the Middle Ages, though even by the end of the fifteenth century it was not yet complete: the twentieth century finds us reaching forward to a new advance. We have spoken of Erasmus' efforts to bring back peace from her exile, of the experiences of his youth when Holland had wept for her children. In 1517, when he wrote his 'Complaint of Peace cast forth from all lands', he was a man and one of Charles' councillors; but Holland was still weeping and refusing comfort. She had good reason. The provinces of the Netherlands were disunited, no sway imposed upon them with strength enough first to restrain and then to knit together. On either side of the Zuider Zee lay two bitter enemies: Holland, which had accepted the

Burgundian yoke, and Friesland, which after a long struggle against foreign domination, had been reduced by the rule of Saxon governors, Duke Albert and Duke George. To the south was Gueldres, which, under its Duke, Charles of Egmont, had thrown in its lot with France against Burgundy, and was continually instigating the subjugated Frieslanders to rebellion. Then was war in the gates.

This was the kind of thing that happened. In 1516, after a fresh outbreak of the ceaseless struggle, Henry of Nassau, Stadhouder of Holland and Zeeland, ordered that all Gueldrians or Frieslanders who showed their faces in his dominions should be put to death; and some who were resident at the Hague were executed on the charge of sending aid to their compatriots. A raid by the Gueldrians ended in the massacre of Nieuwpoort. Nassau replied by ravaging the country up to the walls of Arnhem, the Gueldres capital.

Duke Charles had terrible forces at command. A body of mercenary troops, known as the Black Band, had been used by George of Saxony for the repression of Friesland in 1514, and since then had been seeking employment wherever they could find it. At the same time, one of the conquered Frieslanders, known as Long Peter, had turned to piracy as an effective way of revenging himself on Holland. Proclaiming himself 'King of the Sea', he seized every ship that came in his way, showing no mercy to Hollanders and holding all others to ransom.

In May 1517, the Duke, violating a truce not yet expired, renewed hostilities. The Black Band, some of whom had strayed as far as Rouen in quest of fighting, flocked back. At the end of June 3000 of them crossed the Zuider Zee in Long Peter's ships and disembarked suddenly at Medemblik, in North Holland. The town was quickly set on fire, and everything destroyed except the citadel; the fleet carrying back the first spoils. Then they marched southwards, burning what they list; and happy were those whose offer of ransom was accepted, to escape with plunder only.

There was no fixed plan. The murderous horde wandered along, turning to right or left as fancy suggested. After burning five country towns, they appeared at Alcmar, the chief town of North Holland, into which the most precious possessions of the neighbourhood had been hurriedly conveyed. By a heavy payment, the burghers purchased immunity from the flames; but for eight days the town was given up to the lust and ferocity of an uncontrolled soldiery, from whose senseless destruction it took thirty years to recover. Egmond, with its great abbey, was pillaged; and then it was Haarlem's turn to suffer. But by this time resistance had been organized. Troops had been called back from garrison work in Friesland, and a strong line drawn in front of Haarlem. Headed off, the Black Band turned suddenly away. Passing Amsterdam and Culemborg, it penetrated down into South Holland, whence it would be easy to pass back into Gueldres.

Asperen was its next prey. Three times the citizens beat off the cruel foe: a few more to man their walls, and they might have driven him right away, to overwhelm others less fortunate and less brave.

But it was not to be. At the fourth attempt the marauders were successful, and massacre ensued. Death to the men, worse than death to the women: nor age nor innocence could touch those black hearts. A schoolmaster with his boys fled into a church and hid trembling in the rood-loft. Before long they were discovered. Thirsting for blood, some of the monsters rushed up the steps and tossed the shrieking victims over on to the pikes of their comrades below. When all the butchery was finished, a few helpless and infirm survivors were dragged out of hiding-places. The miserable creatures were driven out of the city and the gates barred in their faces. For a month the Black Band held Asperen as a standing camp, living upon the provisions stored up by the dead. Then Nassau came with troops and drove them forth, pursuing into Gueldres, where he burned '46 good villages' in revenge. The sight of fire blazing to heaven is appalling enough when men are ranged all on one side, and the battle is with the element alone. Our peace-lapped imaginations cannot picture the terror of flames kindled aforethought. As those poor fugitives scattered over the country, cowering into the darkness out of the fire's searching glow, they cannot but have recalled the words: 'Woe unto them that are with child and to them that give suck in those days.' At least they could give thanks that their flight was not in the winter.

Meanwhile Long Peter had not been idle. On 14 August he had a great battle with the Hollanders off Hoorn. Eleven ships he took, and cast their crews into the sea: 500 men, save one, a Gueldrian, struggling in the calm summer waters and stretching out their hands to a foe who knew no pity. In September he surrounded a merchant fleet. The Easterlings escaped at heavy ransom; but the crews of three Holland vessels were flung to the waves. Then he carried the war on to the land, to glean what the Black Band had left. With 1200 men he took Hoorn by escalade; plunder-laden and sated, they returned to the sea. Nothing was too small or too helpless for his rapacity. Along the coast they picked up a barge of Enckhuizen. Its only crew, master and mate, were thrown overboard, and Peter's fleet sailed upon its way. We must remember that the provinces engaged in this internecine strife were not widely diverse in race, and that to-day they are peacefully united under one governance.

The winter of 1517–18 was spent by the Black Band in Friesland. Three thousand men who are prepared to take by force what is not given to them, do not lie hungry in the cold. We may be sure that under them the land had no rest. At Easter they began to move southwards in quest of other victims and other employ. But as they halted between Venlo and Roermond, resistance confronted them. Nassau had arrayed by his side the Archbishop of Cologne and the Dukes of Juliers and Cleves: the gates of the cities were closed and the ferry-boats that would have carried them across the Maas had been kept on the other side. Caught in a trap, the freebooters promised to lay down their weapons and disperse. The disarmament proceeded quietly till one of the company-leaders refused to part with a bombard, the new invention, of which he was very proud. A trumpeter, seeing the man hesitate, sounded a warning, and the containing troops stood on the alert. Readiness led to action. Suddenly they fell on the helpless horde, for whom there was no safety but in flight. A thousand were massacred before Nassau and his confederates could check their men.

Erasmus was about to set out from Louvain to Basle, to work at a new edition of the New Testament. Bands such as these were, of course, a peril to travellers. Half exultant, half disgusted, he wrote to More: 'These fellows were stripped before disbandment: so they will have all the more excuse for fresh plundering. This is consideration for the people! They were so hemmed in that not one of them could have escaped: yet the Dukes were for letting them go scot-free. It was mere chance that any of them were killed. Fortunately, a man blew his trumpet: there was at once an uproar, and more than a thousand were cut down. The Archbishop alone was sound. He said that, priest though he was, if the matter were left to him, he would see that such things should never occur again. The people understand the position, but are obliged to acquiesce.' To Colet he exclaimed more bitterly: 'It is cruel! The nobles care more for these ruffians than for their own subjects. The fact is, they count on them to keep the people down.' Let us be thankful that Europe to-day has no experience of such mercenaries.

A sign of the troubles of the times was the existence of the French order of Trinitarians for the redemption of prisoners. This need had been known even when Rome's power was at its height, for Cicero[1] specifies the redemption of men captured by pirates as one of the ways in which the generously minded were wont to spend their money. The practice lasted down continuously through the Middle Ages. Gaguin, the historian of France, Erasmus' first patron in Paris, was for many years General of the Trinitarians, and made a journey to Granada to redeem prisoners who had been taken fighting against the Moors. Even in the eighteenth century, church offertories in England were asked and given to loose captives out of prison.

Where the king's peace is not kept and the king's writ does not run, men learn to rely on themselves. Those who protect themselves with strength, discover the efficacy of force, and soon are not content to apply it merely on the defensive. It is not surprising, therefore, to find in Erasmus' day many cases of resort to violence to remedy defective titles. Nowadays we never hear of a defeated candidate for

[1] *De Officiis*, 2. 16.

a coveted post trying to obtain by force and right of possession the position which has been given to another. It is unthinkable, for instance, that a Warden of Merton duly elected should have to eject from college some disappointed rival who had possessed himself of the Warden's office and house: as actually happened in 1562. It is, perhaps, not so much that we have become more law-abiding, as that we realize that any such attempt must be fruitless when the strong arm of the State is at hand, ready to assert the rights of the lawful claimant.

In Erasmus' day might was often right. Thus in 1492 the Abbot of St. Bertin's at St. Omer died, and the monks elected in his place a certain James du Val, who was duly consecrated in July 1493. The Bishop of Cambray, however, had had the abbey in his eye for his younger brother Antony, who had been ejected ten years before by the powerful family of Arenberg from the Abbey of St. Trond in Limburg, and meanwhile had been living unemployed at Louvain. The Bishop persuaded the Pope to annul du Val's election and appoint Antony in his place, probably on some technical ground. Armed with this permission he appeared at St. Omer in October 1493 and violently installed his brother; who held the abbey undisturbed till his death nearly forty years later. The Bishop's success with the Pope is the more noteworthy, as for a period of seven years he himself had refused to surrender an abbey near Mons to a papal nominee, who was not strong enough to wrest it from him. Again, during the five years of the English occupation of Tournay, 1513–18, there was a continual struggle between two rival bishops, appointed when the see fell vacant in 1513—Wolsey nominated by Henry VIII and Louis Guillard by the Pope. It goes without saying that Wolsey won; and Guillard did not get in till 1519, the year after the evacuation by the English.

Fernand tells a story of violence at the monastery of Souillac, which was closely connected with his own at Chezal-Benoît. When the Abbot died, a monk of St. Martin's at Tours, who was a native of Souillac, with the aid of a brother who was a court official, got himself put in as abbot before the monks had time to elect. They appealed to the king, but quite in vain; for instead of giving ear to their complaint he sent down a troop of soldiers to support the invading Abbot. It was a grievous time for the poor monks. The garrison did whatever they pleased: imprisoned the faithful servants of the monastery, introduced hunting-dogs and birds, roared out their licentious choruses to the sound of lute and pipe, and gave up the whole day to games of every sort, in which the weaker brethren joined. Those who refused to do so or to violate their vows by eating flesh were insulted; and as they held divine service, coarse laughter and clamour interrupted them. Strict watch was kept upon them, too, lest they should speak or write to any one of their injuries. We need not deplore the passing of such 'good old days'.

It is necessary to realize the certainty which in the

sixteenth century men allowed themselves to feel on subjects of the highest importance; for nothing short of this intense conviction is adequate to explain the ferocity with which they treated those over whom they had triumphed in matters of religion. Burning at the stake was the common method of expiation. The fires of Smithfield consumed brave, humble victims, while Erasmus jested over the rising price of wood. In France the Inquisition entrapped many men of literary distinction, Louis de Berquin 1529, John de Caturce 1532, Stephen Dolet 1546; on the charge of heresy or atheism which could only with great difficulty be refuted. To kill a fellow-creature or to watch him put to death would be physically impossible to most of us, in our unruffled lives; where from year's-end to year's-end we hardly even hear a word spoken in anger. In consequence it is difficult for us to understand the indifference with which in the sixteenth century men of the most advanced refinement regarded the sufferings of others. Between rival combatants and claimants for thrones fierce measures are more intelligible; especially in days when stone walls did not a prison make—such a prison, at least, as the prisoner might not some day hope to break. Things had improved somewhat since the Middle Ages. We hear less of the varieties of mutilation, the blinding, loss of nose, hands, breasts, which were the portion of either sex indiscriminately, when the death-penalty had not been fully earned. But it was still fashionable to suspend your adversary in a cage and torture him, or to confine him for years in a dungeon which light and air could never reach. The executions of heretics became public shows, carefully arranged beforehand, and attended by rank and fashion; to whom to show any sign of sensibility would have been disgrace. Impossible it seems to believe. We must remember that the perpetrators of such noble acts had persuaded themselves that they were serving God. They were as confident as Joshua or as Jehu that they knew His will; and they had no hesitation in carrying it out.

If you may take a man's life in God's name, there can be no objection to telling him a lie. The violation of the safe-conduct which brought Hus to Constance was a fine precedent for breaking faith with a heretic. When Luther came to Worms to answer for himself before Emperor and Diet, the Pope's representatives reminded Charles of the principle which had lighted the fires at Constance and ridded the world of a dangerous fellow. Fortunately Charles had German subjects to consider, and the Germans had a reputation for good faith of which they were proud. Let us credit him too with some generosity; he was scarcely 21, and the young find the arguments of expediency difficult. Anyway, Luther with the help of his friends got off safely. The intrigues and subterfuges of diplomatists are still very often revolting to honest men. But there is some excuse for them; they act on behalf of nations, who have to look to themselves for protection and can rarely afford to be generous and aboveboard. But so barefaced a violation of faith to an individual before the eyes of the world would no longer be tolerated, not even in the name of the Lord.

The following example will illustrate the ideas of the age about the treatment of heretics ; an example of faith continually broken and of incredible cruelty. In 1545 the Cardinal de Tournon and Baron d'Oppède, the first president of the Parliament of Aix, were moved to extirpate that plague-spot of Southern France, the Vaudois communities of Dauphiné, who went on still in their wickedness and heresy. The intriguers prepared a decree revoking the letters patent of 1544, which had suspended proceedings against the Vaudois ; and when the keeper of the seals refused to present it to the king for signature, by unlawful means they presented it through a secretary and unlawfully procured the affixion of the seals. But this was a mere trifle : greater things were to follow.

On 13 April 1545 the Baron entered the Vaudois territory at the head of a body of troops, reinforced by the papal Vice-legate and a fanatical mob of countryfolk. The inhabitants offered little resistance, and soon villages were in flames on every side. At Mérindol the soldiers found only one inhabitant, a poor idiot ; all the rest had fled. The Baron ordered him to be shot. Above by the castle some women were discovered hiding in a church ; after indescribable outrages they were thrown headlong from the rocks. Cabrières being fortified was prepared to stand a siege ; but on a promise of their lives and property the inhabitants opened the gates. Without a moment's hesitation the Baron gave orders to put them all to death. The soldiers refused to break plighted faith; but the mob had no scruples and the ghastly work began. 'A multitude of women and children had fled to the church: the furious horde rushed headlong among them and committed all the crimes of which hell could dream. Other women had hidden themselves in a barn. The Baron caused them to be shut up there and fire set to the four corners. A soldier rushed to save them and opened the door, but the women were driven back into the fire with blows of pikes. Twenty-five women had taken shelter in a cavern at some distance from the town. The Vice-legate caused a great fire to be lighted at the entrance: five years afterwards the bones of the victims were found in the inmost recesses.'[1] La Coste had the same fate; the promise made and immediately violated, and then all the terrors of hell. In the course of a few weeks 3000 men and women were massacred, 256 executed, and six or seven hundred sent to the galleys; while children unnumbered were sold as slaves. The offence of these poor people was that they had been seeking in their own fashion to draw nearer to the God of Love.

But public morals ever lag behind private; and in the sixteenth century private standards of truth and honour were not so high as they are now. Here again we may find one main cause in the absence of personal security. In these days of settled government,

[1] R. C. Christie, *Étienne Dolet*, ch. xxiv.

when thought and speech are free, it is scarcely possible to realize what men's outlook upon life must have been when walls had ears and a man's foes might be those of his own household. In Henry VII's reign England had not had time to forget the Wars of the Roses, and claimants to the throne were still occasionally executed in the Tower. Even under the mighty hand of Henry VIII ministers rose and fell with alarming rapidity. When princes contend, private men do well to hold their peace; lest light utterances be brought up against them so soon as Fortune's wheel has swung to the top those that were underneath. In matters of faith, too, it was supremely necessary to be careful; for unguarded words might arouse suspicions of heresy, to be followed by the frightful penalties with which heresy was extirpated. On great questions, therefore, men must have kept their tongues and thoughts in a strict reserve: candour and openness, those valuable solvents of social humours, can only have been practised by the unwise.

Truth is one of those things in which to him that hath shall be given. It is a common jest in the East that professional witnesses come daily to the law-courts waiting to be hired by either side. The harder truth is to discover, with the less are men content. With many inducements to dissimulation and no great expectations of personal honesty, men are likely to traffic with expediency and to be adept in justifying themselves when they forsake the truth.

Some examples of this may be found in Erasmus'

letters. When he was in Italy in 1509, Henry VII died. His English patron, Lord Mountjoy, was intimate with Henry VIII. A few weeks after the accession a letter from Mountjoy reached Erasmus, inviting him to return to England and promising much in the young king's name. The letter was in fact written by Ammonius, an Italian, who afterwards became Latin secretary to the king. He was recognized as one of the best scholars of the day; and there can be no doubt that the letter was his composition. Mountjoy was a sufficiently keen scholar to sit up late at night over his books, and to be chosen as a companion to the young Prince Henry in his studies; but such autograph letters by him as survive show that he wrote with difficulty even in English, and it is impossible to suppose that he would have kept an accomplished Latinist in his employ merely to act as copyist to his effusions. Moreover, Erasmus, writing a few years later, says that he recognized the letter as Ammonius' work, not from the handwriting, which he had forgotten, but from the style. Nevertheless he allowed it to be published in 1519 as his patron's. Of his connivance in the matter there is actual proof; for in 1517 he had the letter copied by one of his servant-pupils into a letter-book, and added the heading himself. What he first wrote was: 'Andreas Ammonius Erasmo Roterodamo S. D.,' but afterwards he scratched out Ammonius' name and wrote in 'Guilhelmus Montioius'. In a sense, of course, he was correct; for the letter was written in Mountjoy's name. But he cannot have been unaware that in an age which valued elegant Latinity so highly, his patron would be gratified by the ascription.

It was no great matter, and did no harm to any one. But it throws some doubt on Erasmus' statement as to the scholarship of Henry VIII. When Henry's book against Luther appeared in 1521, people said that Erasmus had lent him a hand. In denying the insinuation Erasmus avers that Henry was quite capable of doing the work himself, and adds that his own suspicions of Henry's capacity had been dispelled by Mountjoy, who when tutor to the young prince had preserved rough copies of Latin letters written by Henry's own hand; and these he produced to convince the doubter. Erasmus had a double motive in asserting Henry's authorship, to play the courtier and to avoid provoking Luther; and Mountjoy, as we have seen, is not above suspicion. But there is some further evidence in support of them all, prince and patron and scholar. Pace, Colet's successor at St. Paul's, speaks of hearing Henry talk Latin quickly and readily; and Giustinian, the Venetian ambassador, quotes a few remarks made to him by Henry in Latin by way of greeting. Till more evidence is forthcoming, Erasmus must be let off on this count with a Not proven.

Another example of scant regard for truth is his disowning of the *Julius Exclusus*. This was a witty dialogue, in Erasmus' best style, on the death of Pope Julius II. The Pope is shown arriving at the gate of heaven, accompanied by his Genius, a sort of guardian angel, and amazed to find it locked, with no preparation at all for his reception. His amazement grows when St. Peter at length appears and makes it plain that the gate is not going to be opened, and that there is no room in heaven for Julius with his record of wars and other unchristian deeds; whereupon there is a fine set-to, and each party receives some hard knocks.

That Erasmus was its author there can be no doubt; for there is evidence in two directions of the existence of a copy or copies of it in his handwriting, and we cannot suppose that at that period of his life, when he regularly had one or more servant-pupils in his employ, he would have troubled to copy out with his own hand a work of that length by another. There was nothing very outrageous in the dialogue, nothing much more than there was in the *Moria*; but it was not the sort of thing for a man to write who was so closely connected as Erasmus was with the Papal see, and who wished to stand well with it in the future. The *Julius* appeared in print in 1517, of course anonymously, and Erasmus was pleased with its reception; but he soon found that people who were not in the secret were attributing it to him. That would never do; so he set to work to repudiate it. The friends that knew he exhorted to know nothing; the rest he endeavoured to persuade that he was not the author, using many forms of equivocation. He rises to his greatest heights in addressing cardinals. To Campegio, then in London, he writes on 1 May 1519:

'How malicious some people are! Any scandalous book that comes out they at once put down to me. That silly production, *Nemo*, they said was mine; and people would have believed them, only the author ⟨Hutten⟩ indignantly claimed it as his own. Then those absurd Letters ⟨of the Obscure Men⟩: of course I was thought to have had a hand in them. Finally, they began to say that I was the author of this book of Luther; a person I have hardly ever heard of, certainly I have not read his book. As all these failed, they are trying to fasten on me an anonymous dialogue which appears to make mock of Pope Julius. Five years ago I glanced through it, I can hardly say I read it. Afterwards I found a copy of it in Germany, under various names. Some said it was by a Spaniard, name unknown; others ascribed it to Faustus Andrelinus, others to Hieronymus Balbus. For myself I do not quite know what to think. I have my suspicions; but I haven't yet followed them up to my satisfaction. Certainly whoever wrote it was very foolish;'—that sentence was from his heart!—'but even more to blame is the man who published it. To my surprise some people attribute it to me, merely on the ground of style, when it is nothing like my style, if I am any judge: though it would not be very wonderful if others did write like me, seeing that my books are in all men's hands. I am told that your Reverence is inclined to doubt me: with a few minutes' conversation I am sure I could dispel your suspicions. Let me assure you that books of this kind written by others I have had suppressed: so it is hardly likely that I should have published such a thing myself, or ever wish to publish it.'

Not bad that, from the author of the *Julius*. A fortnight later he wrote to Wolsey to much the same effect, instancing as books that had been attributed to him Hutten's *Nemo* and *Febris*, Mosellanus' *Oratio de trium linguarum ratione*, Fisher's reply to Faber, and even More's *Utopia*. As to the *Julius* he says: 'Plenty of people here will tell you how indignant I was some years ago when I found the book being privately passed about. I glanced through it (I can hardly be said to have read it); and I tried vigorously to get it suppressed. This is the work of the enemies of good learning, to try and fasten this book upon me.' Finally, to clinch his argument, he asseverates with audacious ingenuity: 'I have never written a book, and I never will, to which I will not affix my own name.'

Jortin points out that the only thing which Erasmus specifically denies is the publication of the *Julius*. As we have seen, an author of consequence in those days rarely troubled to correct his own proof-sheets. Erasmus left his *Moria* behind in Paris for Richard Croke to see through the press; More committed his *Utopia* to Erasmus, who had it printed for him at Louvain; Linacre sent his translations of Galen to Paris by the hands of Lupset, who supervised the printing. It is therefore quite probable that Erasmus did not personally superintend the publication of the *Julius*; but until students of typography can tell us definitely which is the first printed edition, and where it was printed, we cannot be certain. But besides this point of practice born of convenience, there was another born of modesty. With compositions that were purely literary—poems and other creations of art and fancy, as opposed to more solid productions—the convention arose of pretending that the publication of them was due to the entreaties of friends, or even in some cases that it had been carried out by ardent admirers without the author's knowledge. Printing, with its ease of multiplication, had made publication a far more definite act than it was in the days of manuscripts. In the prefaces to his early compositions, Erasmus almost always assumes this guise. More actually wrote to Warham and to another friend that the *Utopia* had been printed without his knowledge. Of course this was not true, but nobody misunderstood him. Dolet's *Orationes ad Tholosam* appeared through the hand of a friend, but with the most transparent figments.

There was, therefore, abundant precedent for denying authorship. But there is a difference between the light veil of modesty and clouds of dust raised in apprehension. The publication of the *Julius* certainly placed Erasmus in a dilemma; he extricated himself by equivocation, which barely escapes from direct untruth. It is possible that a public man of his position at the present day might find himself driven to a similar method of escape from a similar indiscretion.[1] But experience has taught men not to write lampoons which they dare not avow, and a more effective law of copyright protects them against publication by pirate printers.

[1] An example of this may be seen in the new *Life of Edward Bulwer, First Lord Lytton*, 1913, ii. 71–6. Bulwer-Lytton's letter, 15 March 1846, denying the authorship of the *New Timon*, might almost have been translated from Erasmus' to Campegio, except that it goes further in falsehood.

VII

PRIVATE LIFE AND MANNERS

An interesting parallel is often drawn between Indian life to-day and the life with which we are familiar in the Bible. The women grinding at the mill, the men who take up their beds and walk, the groups that gather at the well, the potter and his wheel, the marriage-feasts, the waterpots standing ready to be filled, the maimed, the leper, and the blind—all these are everyday sights in the streets and households of modern India.

But we may also make an instructive comparison between India and mediaeval, or even Renaissance, Europe. As soon as one gets away from the railway and the telegraph—indeed even where they have already penetrated—one still finds in India conditions prevailing which continued in Europe beyond the Middle Ages. The customary tie between master and servant, lasting from one generation to another, preserves the community of interest which prevented the feudal bond from being irksome. The modern severance of classes, the modern desire for aloofness, has not yet come. The servants are an integral part of the household, sharing in its ceremonies and festivities, crowding into their master's presence without impairing his privacy, and following him as escort whenever he stirs abroad. The child-marriage which we condemn in modern

India, was frequently practised in Europe in the sixteenth century, when the uncertainty of life made men wish to secure the future of their children so far as they could. The foster-mothers with whom young Mughal princes found a home, whose sons they loved as their own brothers, had their counterpart in these islands as late as the days of the great Lord Cork. Walled cities with crowded houses looking into one another across narrow winding alleys, were an inevitable condition of life in sixteenth-century Europe before strong central government had made it safe to live outside the gates. Even the houses of the great were dark, airless, cramped, with tiny windows and dim, opaque glass; such as one may still see at Compton Castle in Devonshire or the Château des Comtes at Ghent. Communications moved slowly along unmetalled roads or up and down rivers. Carriages with two or four horses were occasionally used; but the ordinary traveller rode on horseback, and needy students coming to a university walked, clubbing together for a packhorse to carry their modest baggage. These are features which may still be matched in many parts of India.

The ravages of plague, the absence of sanitation, the recurrence of famine and war, all combined in sixteenth-century Europe to produce an uncertainty in the tenure of life, which modern India knows only too well from all the causes except the last; but India does not follow Europe in the resulting practice of frequent remarriage on both sides. In Erasmus' day a marriage in which neither side had previously or did subsequently contract a similar relation must have been quite exceptional. A certain German lady, after one ordinary husband, became the wife of three leading Reformers in succession, Oecolampadius, Capito, and Bucer—almost an official position, it would seem. She survived them all, and when Bucer died at Cambridge in 1551, was able to return to Basle, to be buried beside Oecolampadius in the Cathedral. Katherine Parr married four times. To her first husband, who left her a widow at fifteen, she was a second wife; to her second, a third wife; to her third, who was Henry VIII, a sixth; and only her fourth was a bachelor.

The custom of the year's 'doole' after the death of husband or wife was just at this period breaking down. In 1488 Edward IV declined a new marriage for his sister, Margaret of York, the new-made widow of Charles the Bold, on the ground that 'after the usage of our realms no estate or person honourable communeth of marriage within the year of their dool'. But Tudor practice was very different. For Mary, Queen of France, who married her Duke of Suffolk as soon as her six weeks of white mourning were out, there was some excuse of urgency; Henry, too, in his rapid marriage with Jane Seymour had special reasons. But Katherine Parr, when her turn to marry him came, was but a few months a widow; and later, in being on with her old love, Thomas Seymour, when her grim master was only just dead, she had no motive beyond the wishes of lovers long delayed. The Princess Mary, however, considered this latter action highly improper.

John Oporinus (Herbst), the Basle printer (1507–68), had a varied experience; taking four widows to wife. At the age of 20 he married—almost, it seems, out of a sense of duty—the widow of his teacher, Xylotectus of Lucerne; an elderly lady who persecuted him sorely, and once in a passion threw dirty water over him. After eight years, two of which he had spent roving through Germany with Paracelsus, she died, leaving her property to relations. Oporinus' next widow had three children, girls, who grew up to share their mother's expensive tastes. For nearly thirty years their extravagance vexed him, though his wife had tact enough to keep from open quarrels. Then one day he returned from the Frankfort fair to find her dead of the plague. The same visitation, 1564, by carrying off first John Herwagen the younger and then Ulrich Iselin, Professor of Law at Basle, made two more widows, successively to bear Oporinus' name. Herwagen's widow, Elizabeth Holzach, was a sweet woman, but died in the fourth month of her new marriage, 17 July 1565. Iselin's was Faustina, daughter of Boniface Amerbach, born in 1530. To her seven children by Iselin, she added one for Oporinus, Emmanuel, born 25 Jan. 1568; but the father of 60 did not live six months to have pleasure in his firstborn.

With such frequent changes the marriage-tie cannot have given the same personal attachment that is possible at the present day: indeed such unions can scarcely have seemed more lasting than the temporary associations of friends. One need only recall the bargainings that occur in the Paston Letters to realize that there was not much romance about their marriages, at any rate beforehand. Thus wrote Sir John Paston in 1473 of a suitor for his sister Anne: 'As for Yelverton, he said but late that he would have her if she had her money; and else not.'

Thomas More is rightly regarded as a man in whom the spirit burned brighter and clearer than in most of his contemporaries; and yet his matrimonial relations savour more of convenience or even of business than of affection. For his first wife, we are told—and there is no reason to doubt the story—, his fancy had lighted on an Essex girl, the daughter of a country-gentleman; but on visiting her at home he found that she had an elder sister not yet married. Feeling that to have her younger sister married first would be a grief to the elder, he 'inclined his affection' towards her and made her his wife in place of his first choice. The interpretation that when he saw the elder sister, he preferred her before the other, might be probable to-day: to apply it to the story of More would be a case of that commonest of 'vulgar errors' in history,—judging the past by the ideas of the present. For five or six years More lived with his girl-bride, whose country training and unformed mind caused much trouble and difficulty to them both. The unequal relation between them appears in a story told by Erasmus; that More delighted her once by bringing home a present of sham jewels, and apparently did not think it necessary to undeceive her about them. Happiness came in time; but after bearing him four children, she died. Within a month the widower came to his father-confessor by night and obtained leave to be married next morning. His new wife was a middle-aged lady of no charms —indeed she seems to have been a regular shrew— who served him as a capable housekeeper and looked after his children while they were young. But she never engaged his affections; and it was his eldest daughter, Margaret, who became the chosen partner of his joys and sorrows in later years.

The habitual remarriage of widows proceeded in part from the desire, or even need, for a husband's protection; and in consequence it was not only the young who were open to men's addresses. Beatus Rhenanus, writing to a servant-pupil who had recently left him to launch forth into the world, counsels him to marry, if possible, a rich and elderly widow; in order that in a few years by her death he may find himself equipped with an ample capital for his real start in life. Such advice from a man like Beatus can only have been in jest: but if there had not been some reality of actual practice, the jest would have fallen flat. Indeed Beatus goes on to indicate that this course had been taken by Reuchlin; whose elderly consort was, however, disobliging enough to live for many years. The ill-success attending Oporinus' essay in this direction we have already seen.

But it was not so with all. Not infrequently Erasmus deplores the imprudence of the young men who had left his service, in allowing themselves to fall in love and marry without securing proper dowries with their young brides. He was indeed, considering his natural shrewdness, singularly ignorant of women; as his advice to youthful husbands sometimes shows. To one, for example, who had written to announce that before long he hoped to become a father, he replies with congratulations, and then says: 'Now that your wife no longer needs your care, you will be able to betake yourself to a university and finish your studies'—advice which we may surely suppose was not taken.

During the insecurity of the Middle Ages, the seclusion of women for their own protection had been severely necessary. In the East the 'purdah-system' reached the length of excluding women of the better classes from the society of all men but those of their own family. Of such rigidity in Europe I cannot find any traces except under Oriental influence;[1] but there is no doubt that women's life at the beginning of the Renaissance in the North was circumscribed. Such higher education as they received was given at home, by father or brothers or husband, or by private tutors. But there are not a few examples of educated women. In the well-known Frisian family, the Canters of Groningen,

[1] In 1729 the Abbé Fourmont found the seclusion of women extensively practised in Athens for fear of the Turks; see R. C. Christie, *Essays and Papers*, p. 69.

parents and children and even the maidservant are said to have spoken regularly in Latin. Antony Vrye of Soest, one of the Adwert circle, wrote to his wife in Latin; and his daughter helped him with the teaching of Latin in the various schools over which he presided, at Campen and Amsterdam and Alcmar. Pirckheimer's sisters and daughters, Peutinger's wife, are famous for their learning. In England throughout the Renaissance period the position of women and their education steadily improved. Alice, Duchess of Suffolk, the foundress of Ewelme, had an interest in literature; and the great Lady Margaret, besides the endowments which are her memorial at the universities, constantly fostered the efforts of Wynkyn de Worde, and herself translated part of the *Imitatio* from the French. The Princess Mary, as the result of the liberal training of Vives and other masters, could translate from Aquinas, take part in acting a play of Terence, and read the letters of Jerome; and before she was 30, made a translation of Erasmus' Paraphrase of St. John's Gospel, which formed part of the English version of those Paraphrases ordered by Injunctions of Edward VI to be placed beside the Bible in every parish church throughout the realm.

More, for his dear 'school', engaged the best teachers he could find. John Clement, afterwards Wolsey's first Reader in Humanity at Oxford, and William Gonell, Erasmus' friend at Cambridge, read Sallust and Livy with them. Nicholas Kratzer, the Bavarian mathematician, also one of Wolsey's

Readers at Oxford, taught them astronomy: to know the pole-star and the dog, and to contemplate the 'high wonders of that mighty and eternal workman',whom More could feel revealed himself also to some 'good old idolater watching and worshipping the man in the moon every frosty night'.[1] Richard Hyrde, the friend of Gardiner and translator of Vives' *Instruction of a Christian Woman*, continued the work after the 'school' had been moved to Chelsea;[2] and when Margaret, eldest and best-beloved scholar, was married. Not that this interfered. The love of learning once implanted brought her with her husband to keep her place among her sisters in that bright Academy. Her fame is well known, how the Bishop of Exeter sent her a gold coin of Portugal in reward for an elegant epistle; how familiarly she corresponded with Erasmus; how she emended the text of Cyprian, imitated the Declamations of Quintilian, and translated the Ecclesiastical History of Eusebius.

It is evident that in England, for women as well as men, the seed of the Renaissance had fallen on good ground. By the middle of the century the gates of the kingdom of knowledge were open, and the thoughtful were rejoicing in the infinite variety of their Paradise regained. In 1547–8, Nicholas Udall, in a preface for Mary's translation of Erasmus' Paraphrase, writes with enthusiasm: 'Neither is it now any

[1] More, *English Works*, 1557, f. 154 E.

[2] See F. Watson, *Vives and the Renascence Education of Women*, 1912.

strange thing to hear gentlewomen, instead of most vain communication about the moon shining in the water, to use grave and substantial talk in Greek or Latin with their husbands in godly matters. It is now no news in England to see young damsels in noble houses and in the courts of princes, instead of cards and other instruments of vain trifling, to have continually in their hands either Psalms, "Omelies" and other devout meditations, or else Paul's Epistles or some book of Holy Scripture matters, and as familiarly both to read and reason thereof in Greek, Latin, French or Italian as in English. It is now a common thing to see young virgins so "nouzled" and trained in the study of letters that they willingly set all other vain pastimes at nought for learning's sake.' It is melancholy to reflect how soon the gates of the kingdom were to be closed again, and its trees guarded by the flaming sword of theological certainty mistaking itself for truth.

Besides marriage, almost the only vocation open to women in the fifteenth century was the monastic life. It was not uncommon for several daughters in a family to embrace religion: parents, apart from higher considerations, regarding it as a sure method of providing for girls who did not wish to marry, or for whom they could not find husbands. As heads of religious houses women held positions of great dignity and influence, and discharged their duties worthily. Within convent walls, too, it was possible for some women to become learned; though in later times the achievements of Diemudis were never rivalled. She was a nun at Wessobrunn in Bavaria at the end of the eleventh century, and during her cloistered life her active pen wrote out 47 volumes, including two complete Bibles, one of which was given in exchange for an estate.

We also hear of women of means, usually widows, dispensing hospitality on a large scale to the needy and deserving. Wessel of Groningen, as we saw, was adopted by a wealthy matron, who saw him shivering in the street on a winter's day and fetched him into her house to warm. Erasmus describes to us a Gouda lady, Berta de Heyen, whose kindness he repeatedly enjoyed in his early years; and in addition to her general charities mentions that she was wont to look out for promising boys in the town school who were designing to enter the Church, receive them into her family amongst her own children, and when their courses were completed, bestir herself to procure them benefices—an indication of the possession of influence outside her own home. He goes on to say that when widowhood came to her, she refused to think of a second marriage, and almost rejoiced to be released from the bonds of matrimony, because she found herself free to practise her liberality. But we must not lay too much stress on these latter utterances. They come from a funeral oration composed after the good lady's death, and addressed to her children, some of whom were nuns: to whom therefore the conventional representation of the Church's attitude towards marriage would be acceptable. Butzbach describes the wife of a wealthy citizen of Deventer as entertaining daily six or seven of the poorer clergy at her table, besides the alms that she distributed continually before her own door. To him she frequently gave food and clothes and money, with much sympathy.

It is noticeable how the charity is represented as proceeding from the wife and not from the husband. A mediaeval moralist urges wives to make good their husbands' deficiencies in this respect; and against the remark Ulrich Ellenbog, the father, notes that he had always left this burden to his wife. The inference is probable that though the sphere of women was in many ways restricted, they were within their own dominion, the household, supreme—more so perhaps than they are to-day. Yet in spite of this domestic authority, I do not see how we can escape the conclusion that the real power rested with the husband, when we read such passages as this in the *Utopia*, where, speaking of punishment, More says: 'Parents chastise their children, husbands their wives.' Indeed, it was recognized as one of the primary duties of a husband, to see that his wife behaved properly.

What we have been saying may be well illustrated by the letter just alluded to from Antony Vrye 'to his dear wife, Berta of Groningen'. It was written 'from Cologne in haste'; and as it appears in Vrye's *Epistolarum Compendium*, it may be dated *c.* 1477. 'Your letter was most welcome, and relieved me of anxiety about you all. I rejoice to hear that the children are well and yourself; your mother too and the whole household. You write that you are expecting me to return by 1 March, to relieve you of all your cares. I wish indeed that I could; but besides our own private matters, there is some public business for me to discharge, and this will take time. So be diligent to look after our affairs, and pray to God to keep you in health and free from fault: my prolonged absence will make my return all the more joyful. It is great pain to me to be absent from you so long, who art all my life and happiness. But as I must, it falls to you to guard our honour and property, and to care for our family. This, Jerome says, is the part of a prudent housewife, and to cherish her own chastity. Bide then at home, most loving wife, and be not tempted by such amusements as delight the vulgar; but patiently and modestly await my return. I too will be a faithful husband to you in everything. Be a chaste and honoured mother to our boy and little girls; and cherish your mother in return for the singular kindness she has showed us.'

One feature of life at this time which materially affected the lives of women, was the length of families and the accompanying infant mortality. It was common enough in all classes down to the middle of the last century; and it is still only too common among the poor. On the walls of churches, more especially in towns, one frequently sees tablets with long lists of children who seem to have been born only to die: and yet the parents went on their way unthinking, and content if from their annual harvest an occasional son or daughter grew up to bless them. Examples of this may be collected on every side. Colet (1467–1519), for instance, was the eldest of twenty-two sons and daughters; and by 1499 he was the only child left to his parents. His father, who was twice Lord Mayor of London, lived till 1510; the mother of this great brood survived them all, and, so far as Erasmus knew, was still living in 1521.

Another case which may be cited is that of Anthony Koberger, the celebrated Nuremberg printer, 1440–1513: and it is the more interesting, since owing to his care for genealogy, we have accurate records of his two marriages and his twenty-five children. The first marriage produced eight, born between 1470 and 1483; of these, three daughters lived to grow up and marry, but of the remaining five—including three sons, all named Anthony, a fact which tells its own tale—none reached a greater age than twelve years. In September 1491 the first wife died; and in August 1492—without observing the full year's 'doole'—Anthony married again, the second wife being herself the sixteenth child of her parents. At first there was only disappointment; in 3½ years four children were born and died, two of these being twins. But better times followed: of the remaining thirteen only three died as infants. Anthony the fifth and John the third, and three sons named after the three kings, Caspar, Melchior and Balthasar, were more fortunate. When 21 years had brought 17 children, the sequence ended abruptly with the death of Anthony the father; leaving, out of the 25 he had received, only 13 children to speak with his enemies in the gate.

A family Bible now in the Bodleian[1] enumerates 16 children born to the same parents in 24 years, 1550–74. One girl was married before she was 16; one son at 20 died of exposure on his way home from Holland; two reached 10, one 8, one 6. None of the remainder ten lived for one year.

Of public morals in the special sense of the term this is not the place to speak in detail. But it may suitably be stated that sixteenth-century standards in these matters were not so high as those of the present day. 'If gold ruste, what shal iren do?' The highest ecclesiastical authorities were unable to check a nominally celibate priesthood from maintaining women-housekeepers who bore them families of children and were in many cases decent and respectable wives to them in all but name; indeed in Friesland the laity for obvious reasons insisted upon this violation of clerical vows. A letter from Zwingli, the Reformer, written in 1518 when he was parish priest of Glarus, gives an astonishing view of his own practice. Under such circumstances we need not wonder that the standards of the laity were low. The highest record that I have met with is that of a Flemish nobleman, who in addition to a large family including a Bishop of Cambray

[1] Biblia Latina, 1529, c. 2.

and an Abbot of St. Omer, is said to have been also the father of 36 bastards. Thomas More as a young man was not blameless. But it is surprising to find that Erasmus in writing an appreciation of More in 1519, when he was already a judge of the King's Bench, stated the fact in quite explicit, though graceful, language; and further, that More took no exception to the statement, which was repeated in edition after edition. We can hardly imagine such a passage being inserted in a modern biography of a public character, even if it were written after his death. Just about the same time More published among his epigrams some light-hearted Latin poems—doubtless written in his youth—such as no public man with any regard for his character would care to put his name to to-day.

There is another matter to which some allusion must be made, the grossness of the age, though here again detail is scarcely possible. The conditions of life in the sixteenth century made it difficult to draw a veil over the less pleasant side of human existence. The houses were filthy; the streets so disgusting that on days when there was no wind to disperse the mephitic vapours, prudent people kept their windows shut. Dead bodies and lacerated limbs must have been frequent sights. Under these circumstances we need not be surprised that men spoke more plainly to one another and even to women than they do now. Sir John Paston's conversations with the Duchess of Norfolk would make less than duchesses blush now. The tales that Erasmus introduces into his writings, the jests of his Colloquies, are often quite unnecessarily coarse; but one which will illustrate our point may be repeated. One winter's morning a stately matron entered St. Gudule's at Brussels to attend mass. The heels of her shoes were caked with snow, and on the smooth pavement of the church she slipped up. As she fell, there escaped from her lips a single word, of mere obscenity. The bystanders helped her to her feet, and amid their laughter she slunk away, crimson with mortification, to hide herself in the crowd. Nowadays great ladies have not such words at command.

Theological controversy has a proverbial name for ferocity; in the sixteenth century other qualities were added to this. In 1519 a young Englishman named Lee, who was afterwards Archbishop of York, ventured to criticize Erasmus' New Testament, with a vehemence which under the circumstances was perhaps unsuitable. Erasmus of course resented this; and his friends, to cool their indignation, wrote and published a series of letters addressed to the offender: 'the Letters of some erudite men, from which it is plain how great is the virulence of Lee.' Among the contributors was Sapidus, head master of the famous school at Schlettstadt, which was one of the first Latin schools of the age. His letter to Lee concludes with a disgusting piece of imagery, which would shock one if it proceeded from the most unpleasantly minded schoolboy. One cannot conceive a Head Master of Rugby appearing in print in such a way now.

VIII

THE POINT OF VIEW

THERE is one thing in the world which is constantly with us, and which has probably continued unchanged throughout all ages of history: the weather. Yet Erasmus' writings contain no traces of that delight in brilliant sunshine which most Northerners feel, nor of that wonder at the beauties of the firmament which was so real to Homer. He frequently remarks that the weather was pestilent, that the winds blew and ceased not, that the sea was detestably rough and the clouds everlasting; but of the praise which accompanies enjoyment there is scarcely a word. His utmost is to say that the climate of a place is salubrious. He often describes his journeys. As he rode on horseback across the Alps or was carried down the Rhine in a boat, he must have had ample opportunity to behold the glories which Nature sometimes spreads before us in our Northern clime, and lavishes more constantly on less favoured regions. But the loveliness of blue skies and serene air, the glitter of distant snows, the soft radiance of the summer moon, and the golden architrave of the sunset he had no eyes to see.

Such indifference to the beauties of Nature admits, however, of some explanation. With a scantier population than that which now covers the earth, there was less agriculture and more of waste and unkempt places not yet reduced to the service of mankind. Solitudes were vaster and more complete. In a country so well cared for as England is to-day, it is difficult to imagine how unpleasing can be the aspect of land over which Nature still has the upper hand, how desolate and dreadful the great mountain areas which men now have to seek at the ends of the earth, where the smoke rises not and even the lone goatherd has not penetrated. To-day our difficulty is to escape from the thronging pressure of millions: we rarely experience what in the sixteenth century must often have been felt—the shrinking to leave, the joy of returning to, the kindly race of men. Ascham in the *Toxophilus* (1545), when discussing the relaxations open to the scholar who has been 'sore at his book', urges that 'walking alone into the field hath no token of courage in it'. But though this may have been true by that time in the immediate neighbourhood of English towns, it was not yet true abroad; for Thomas Starkey in his *Dialogue* (1538), almost as valuable a source as the *Utopia*, praises foreign cities with their resident nobles by comparison with English, which are neglected and dirty 'because gentlemen fly into the country to live, and let cities, castles and towns fall into ruin and decay'.

It is tantalizing, too, considering how abundant are Erasmus' literary remains, that we get so little description of places from him. He travelled far and wide, in the Low Countries, up and down the

Rhine, through France, southwards to Rome and Naples. He was a year in Venice, three years at Cambridge, eight years at Basle, six at Freiburg. What precious information he might have given us about these places, which then as now were full of interesting buildings and treasures of art! what a mine of antiquarian detail, if he had expatiated occasionally! But a meagre description of Constance, a word or two about Basle in narrating an explosion there, glimpses of Walsingham and Canterbury in his colloquy on pilgrimages—that is almost all that can be culled from his works about the places he visited. When he came to Oxford, Merton tower had been gladdening men's eyes for scarcely fifty years, and the tower of Magdalen had just risen to rival its beauty; Duke Humfrey's Library and the Divinity School were still in their first glory, and the monks of St. Frideswide were contemplating transforming the choir of their church into the splendid Perpendicular such as Bray had achieved at Westminster and Windsor for Henry VII. But Erasmus tells us nothing of what he saw; only what he heard and said. This lack of enjoyment in Nature, lack of interest in topography and archaeology, was probably personal to him. It was not so with some of his friends. More and Ellenbog, as we have seen, could feel the beauty in the night

> 'Of cloudless climes and starry skies'.

Aleander in a diary records the exceptional brilliance of the planet Jupiter at the end of September 1513.

He pointed it out to his pupils in the Collège de la Marche at Paris, and together they remarked that its rays were strong enough to cast a shadow. Ellenbog enjoyed the country, and Luther also was susceptible to its charms. Budaeus had a villa to which he delighted to escape from Paris, and where he laid out a fine estate. Beatus Rhenanus after thirty years retained impressions of Louis XII's gardens at Tours and Blois and of a 'hanging garden' in Paris; and could write a detailed account of the Fugger palace at Augsburg with its art treasures. Or think of the painters. The Flemings of the fifteenth century had learnt from the Italians to fit into their pictures landscapes seen through doors or windows, gleaming in sunshine, green and bright. Van Eyck's 'Adoration of the Lamb' is set in beautiful scenery; grassy slopes and banks studded with flowers, soft swelling hills, and blue distances crowned with the towers he knew so well, Utrecht and Maestricht and Cologne and Bruges. Even in the interiors of Durer and Holbein, where no window opens to let in the view, Nature is not left wholly unrepresented; for flowers often stand upon the tables, carnations and lilies and roses, arranged with taste and elegance. On the whole the enjoyment of Nature formed but a small part in the outlook of that age as compared with the prominence it receives in modern literature and life; but we should be wrong in inferring that it was wholly absent.

To the men of the fifteenth century the earth

was still the centre of the universe: the sun moved round it like a more magnificent planet, and the stars had been created

> 'to shed down
> Their stellar influence on all kinds that grow'.

Aristarchus had seen the truth, though he could not establish it, in the third century B.C. But Greek science had been forgotten in an age which knew no Greek; and it was not till after Erasmus' death that an obscure canon in a small Prussian town near Danzig—Nicholas Copernicus, 1473–1543—found out anew the secret of the world. This fruit of long cold watches on the tower of his church he printed with full demonstration, but he scarcely dared to publish the book: indeed a perfect copy only reached him a few days before his death. Even in the next century Galileo had to face imprisonment and threats of torture, because he would speak that which he knew. But when Erasmus was born, the earth itself was but partially revealed. Men knew not even whether it were round or flat; and the unplumbed sea could still estrange. The voyages of the Vikings had passed out of mind, and the eyes of Columbus and Vespucci had not yet seen the limits of that western ocean which so long fascinated their gaze. Polo had roamed far into the East; but as yet Diaz and da Gama had not crowned the hopes which so often drew Henry the Navigator to his Portuguese headland.

In the world of thought the conception of

uniformity in Nature, though formed and to some extent accepted among the advanced, was still quite outside the ordinary mind. Miracles were an indispensable adjunct to the equipment of every saint; and might even be wrought by mere men, with the aid of the black arts. The Devil was an ever-present personality, going about to entrap and destroy the unwary. Clear-minded Luther held converse with him in his cell; and lesser demons were seen or suspected on every side. Thus in 1523 the Earl of Surrey writes to Wolsey describing a night attack on Jedburgh in a Border foray. The horses took fright, and their sudden panic threw all things into confusion. 'I dare not write', he says, 'the wonders that my Lord Dacre and all his company do say they saw that night, six times, of spirits and fearful sights. And universally all their company say plainly the Devil was that night among them six times.' In that gaunt and bleak Border country the traveller overtaken by night may feel a disquieting awe even in these days when the rising moon is no longer a lamp to guide enemies to the attack. Four hundred years ago, when it lay blood-stained and scarred with a thousand fights, bearing no crops to be fired, no homesteads to be sacked, we need not wonder if teams of demons swept down in the darkness and drove through and through the trembling ranks.

Again, in 1552 Melanchthon writes thus to a friend: 'In some cases no doubt the causes of madness and derangement are purely physical; but it is also quite certain that at times men's bodies are entered by devils who produce frenzies prognosticating things to come. Twelve years ago there was a woman in Saxony who had no learning of books, and yet, when she was vexed by a devil, after her paroxysms uttered Greek and Latin prophecies of the war that should be there. In Italy, too, I am told there was a woman, also quite unlearned, who during one of her devilish torments was asked what is the best line of Virgil, and replied, "Learn justice and to reverence the gods" '.[1] In this second case it would seem that the Devil scarcely knew his own business.

Sudden death descending upon the wicked was a judgement of heaven, letting loose the powers of hell; and if the face of the corpse chanced to turn black, there was never any doubt but that Satan had flown off with the soul. Suspicions and accusations of witchcraft were rife; and an old woman had to be careful of the reputation of her cat. Wanderers among the mountains saw dragons; in the forests elves peeped at the woodmen from behind the trees, and fairies danced beneath the moon in the open places. The world had not been sufficiently explored for the absence of contrary experience to carry much weight; and the means for the dissemination of news were quite inadequate. In consequence men had not learnt to doubt the evidence of their senses and to regard things as too strange to be true. It was felt that anything might happen; and as a result almost everything did happen.

[1] *Aen.* 6. 620.

For example, in 1500 there was an outbreak of crosses in two villages not far from Sponheim; and next year the same thing happened at Liège. They appeared on any clothing that was light enough of hue; coloured crosses that no washing or treatment could remove. Men opened their coats to find crosses on their shirts: a woman would look down at her apron, and there, sure enough, was a cross. Clothes that had been folded up and put away in presses, came out with the sacred sign upon them. One day during the singing of the mass thirty men suddenly found themselves marked with crosses. They lasted for nine or ten days, and then gradually faded. It was afterwards remarked that where the crosses had been, the plague followed. Such is Trithemius' account in his chronicle: we may wonder how closely he had questioned his informants.

It is difficult for us to conceive a world in which news spreads mainly by word of mouth. Morning and evening it is poured forth to us, by many different agencies, in the daily press; and though many of these succumb to the temptation to be sensational, among the better sort there is a healthy rivalry which restrains exuberance and promotes accuracy. There is safety, too, in numbers. News which appears in one paper only, is looked at doubtfully until it is confirmed by the rest; but even unanimity amongst all papers will scarcely at first win acceptance for what is at all startling and out of the common, until time and the absence of contradiction may perhaps corroborate. In practice men of credit have learnt not to see the sea-serpent. For a picture of conditions in the sixteenth century we must sweep all the newspapers away. Kings had their heralds and towns their public messengers who took and of course brought back news. Caravans of merchants travelled along the great trade-routes; and their tongues and ears were not idle. Private persons, too, sent their servants on journeys to carry letters. But even so news had to travel by word of mouth; for even when letters were sent, we may be sure that any public news of importance beneath the seals and wafers had reached the bearers also.

But for what they told confirmation was not to be had for the asking. Not till chance brought further messengers was it possible to establish or contradict, and till then the first news held the field. Rumour stalked gigantic over the earth, often spreading falsehood and capturing belief, rarely, as in Indian bazars to-day, with mysterious swiftness forestalling the truth. In such a world caution seems the prime necessity; but men grow tired of caution when events are moving fast and the air is full of 'flying tales'. The general tendency was for them, if not to believe, at any rate to pass on, unverified reports, from the impossibility of reaching certainty. In such a world of bewilderment, sobriety of judgement does not thrive.

Two examples may show the difficulty of learning the truth. In 1477 Charles the Bold was killed at Nancy. That great Duke of Burgundy was not a person to be hidden under a bed. Yet nearly six years later reports were current that he had escaped from the battle and was in concealment. Again, Erasmus, during his residence at Bologna in 1507, made many friends. One of these was Paul Bombasius, a native of that town, who became secretary to Cardinal Pucci, and lost his life at Rome in May 1527, when the city was sacked by Charles v's troops; another was the delightful John de Pins, afterwards diplomatist and Bishop of Rieux. To him in 1532 Erasmus wrote asking for news of Bombasius. The Bishop replied that he had heard a rumour of his death, but hoped it was not true. Not till May 1535 could Erasmus report the result of inquiries made through a friend visiting Bologna, that Bombasius had fallen a victim to the Bourbon soldiery eight years before.

That the movements of the stars should affect human life is not easy to disprove even now, to any one who is determined to maintain the possibility of it; but under the training of modern science scarcely any one retains such a belief. Of the influence formerly attributed to the planets, traces survive in such epithets as mercurial, jovial, saturnine. Comets appearing in the sky caused widespread alarm, and any disasters that followed close were confidently connected with them. The most learned scientists observed the stars and cast horoscopes: Cardan, for instance, published a collection of the horoscopes of great men. The Church looked askance on astrology, suspecting it of connexion with forbidden arts; but it could not check the observance of lucky days and the warnings of the heavens. Even a Pope himself, Julius II, deferred his coronation until the stars were in a fortunate conjunction.

Every university student should be familiar with the story of Anthony Dalaber, undergraduate of St. Alban's Hall in Oxford, which Froude introduced into his *History of England* from Foxe's *Book of Martyrs*; it is the most vivid picture we have of university life in the early sixteenth century. Dalaber was one of a company of young men who were reading Lutheran books at Oxford. Wolsey, wishing to check this, had sent down orders in February 1528 to arrest a certain Master Garret, who was abetting them in the dissemination of heresy. The Vice-Chancellor, who was the Rector of Lincoln, seized Dalaber and put him in the stocks, but was too late for Garret, who had made off into Dorsetshire. He took counsel with the Warden of New College and with the Dean of Wolsey's new foundation, Cardinal College; and at length, as they could find out nothing, being 'in extreme pensiveness', they determined to consult an astrologer. They knew they were doing wrong. Such inquiries were forbidden by the law of the Church, and they were afraid; but they were more afraid of Wolsey. The man of science drew a figure upon the floor of his secret chamber, and made his calculations; at the end he reported that the fugitive was fled in a tawny coat to the South-east. The trembling officials hastily dispatched messengers to have the ports watched in Kent and Sussex, hoping that their transgression might at least be justified by success. They were successful: Master Garret *was* caught—trying to take ship at Bristol. It would need awesome circumstances indeed to send a modern Vice-Chancellor through the night to inquire of an astrologer.

In the realm of medicine, too, magic and the supernatural had great weight, and claimed a measure of success which is not unintelligible in these days, when the value of the will as an ally in healing is being understood. Erasmus, suffering from the stone, was presented by a Hungarian physician with an astrological mug, shaped like a lion, which was to cure his trouble. He used it and felt better, but was not sure how much to attribute to the lion. The famous Linacre, one of the founders of the College of Physicians, sent to Budaeus, a French court official and the first Greek scholar of the age, one gold ring and eighteen silver rings which had been blessed by Henry VIII, and had thus been made preservative against convulsions; and Budaeus presented them to his womenkind. We need not take this to imply that he thought little of them; more probably he reflected that convulsions are most frequent among the race of babies, and therefore distributed them where they would be most useful. Anyway, it was Linacre who sent them. With such notions abroad, quackery must have been rife, and serious medical practitioners had many difficulties to contend with. Some idea of these may be gained from a letter written by Wolfgang Rychard, a physician of high repute at Ulm, to a friend at Erfurt, whither he was thinking of sending his son to practise. He asks his friend to inquire of the apothecaries what was the status of doctors, whether they were allowed by the town council to hire houses for themselves and to live freely without exactions, as at Tubingen and universities in the South, or whether they were obliged to pay an annual fee to the town, before they might serve mankind with their healing art.

The feeble-minded and half-witted are nowadays caught up into asylums, for better care, and to ensure that their trouble dies with them. Of old it was thought that God gave them some recompense for their affliction by putting into their mouths truths and prophecies which were hidden from the wise; and thus the village soothsayer or witch often held a strong position in local politics. But it is surprising to find the Cardinal of Sion, Schinner, a clever and experienced diplomatist, writing in 1516, with complete seriousness: 'A Swiss idiot, who prophesies many true things, has foretold that the French will suffer a heavy blow next month'; as though the intelligence would really be of value to his correspondent.

But the prophet's credit varied with his circumstances. Early in the sixteenth century a Franciscan friar, naming himself Thomas of Illyria, wandered about through Southern France, calling on men to repent and rebuking the comfortable vices of the clergy. A wave of serious thought spread with him, and all the accompaniments of a religious revival, such as the twentieth century saw lately in Wales. As the 'saintly man' set foot in villages and towns, games and pleasures were suddenly abandoned, and the churches thronged to overflowing. His words were gathered up, especially those with which he wept over Guienne, that 'fair and delicious province, the Paradise of the world', and foretold the coming of foes who should burn the churches round Bordeaux while the townsmen looked on helplessly from their walls. For a time he retired to a hermitage on a headland by Arcachon, where miracles were quickly ascribed to him. An image of the Virgin was washed ashore, to be the protectress of his chapel. His prayers, and a cross drawn upon the sand, availed to rescue a ship that was in peril on the sea. When English pirates had plundered his shrine, the waves opened and swallowed them up. Later on he withdrew to Rome, where he won the confidence of Clement VII, and he died at Mentone. But his fame remained great in Guienne. Half a century onward, during the war of 1570, when from Bordeaux men saw the church of Lormont across the river burning in the name of religion, the old folks shook their heads and recalled the words of the saintly Thomas.

Less fortunate was a young Franconian herdsman, John Beheim, of Niklashausen—a 'poor illiterate', Trithemius calls him. In the summer of 1476, as he watched his flocks in the fields, he had a vision of the gracious Mother of God, who bade him preach repentance to the people. His fame soon spread, and multitudes gathered from great distances to hear him. The nearest knelt to entreat his blessing, those further off pressed up to touch him, and if possible, snatched off pieces of his garments, till he was driven to speak from an upper window. But his way was not plain. Instigated seemingly by others, he began to touch things social: taxes should not be paid to princes, nor tithes to clergy; rivers and forests were God's common gifts to men, where all might fish or hunt at will. Such words were not to be borne. The Bishop of Wurzburg, his diocesan, took counsel with the Archbishop of Mainz; and the prophet was ordered to be burnt. But death only increased his fame. Still greater crowds flocked to visit the scene of his holy life, until in January 1477 the Archbishop had the church of Niklashausen razed to the ground as the only means of suppressing this popular canonization.

We make a great mistake if we allow ourselves to suppose that because that age knew less than ours, because its bounds were narrower and the undispelled clouds lower down, it therefore thought itself feeble and purblind. By contrast with the strenuous hurry-push of modern life such movement as we can see, looking backwards, seems slow and uncertain of its aim; before the power of modern armaments how helpless all the might of Rome! It is easy to fall into the idea that our mediaeval forefathers moved in the awkward attitudes of pre-Raphaelite painting, that their speech sounded as quaint to them as it does to us now, and that it was hardly possible for them to take life seriously. But in fact each age is to itself modern, progressive, up-to-date; the strong and active pushing their way forward, impatient of trifling, and carrying their fellows with them. A future age that has leapt from one planet to another, or even from one system to another sun and its dependants, that has 'called forth Mazzaroth in his seasons, and loosed the bands of Orion', that has covered the earth with peace as with a garment and pierced the veil that cuts us off from the dead, will look back to us as groping blindly in darkness. But they will be wrong indeed if they think that we realize our blindness.

A still greater pitfall before us is that we read history not as men, but as gods, knowing the event. The name of Marathon to us implies not struggle, not danger, but triumph; and as we think of the little band of Athenians defiling from the mountains and looking on the sea, with the utmost determination we cannot quite enter into their thoughts. Of how little avail must have seemed this handful of lives, their last and best gift to Athens, against the might and majesty of Persia afloat before them. We know of that runner and of the rejoicing that broke out upon his words; and at the very opening of the scene the darkness is pierced by a gleam they could not see, a gleam which for us will not go out. Or think of Edwardes besieging the Sikhs in Multan with his puny force, half of whom, when he began, were in sympathy with the besieged. We know that the terrier's courage kept the tiger in; and, conscious of that, we cannot really place ourselves beside the young Engineer of 29, as with only one or two volunteers of his own race round him he kept the field during those four burning months in which British troops were not allowed to move. The tiger's paw had crushed those whom he had hastened to avenge: he did not know, as we know, that it was not to fall on him too.

There is the same difficulty with the course of years. With the history of four centuries before our minds, only by sustained effort of thought can we realize that the men of 1514 looked onward to 1600, as we to-day look towards 2000, as to a misty blank. We hardly trouble our heads with the future. The air is full of speculations, of attempts to forecast coming developments, the growth, the improvement that is to be. But we do not really look forward, more than a little way. The darkness is too dense: and besides, the needs of the present are very urgent. As we think of the sixteenth century, behind Henry VIII's breach with Rome, behind Edward VI's prayer-books, waits the figure of Pole, steadfast, biding his time; coming to salute Mary with the words of the angel to the Virgin; coming, as he hoped, to set things right for ever. And behind Pole are the Elizabethan settlement and the Puritans; ineradicable from our consciousness. To the Englishmen of 1514 Henry VIII was the divine young king whose prowess at Tournay, whose victory at Flodden seemed to his happy bride the reward of his piety: the name of Luther was unknown: Pole was an unconsidered child. Into their minds we cannot really enter unless we can think away everything that has happened since and call up a mist over the face of time.

IX

PILGRIMAGES

To go on pilgrimage is an instinct which appears in most religions and at all ages. The idea underlying the practice seems to be that God is more nigh in some spots than in others, the desire to seek Him in a place where He may be found: for where God is, there men hope to win remission of sins. So widespread is this sentiment that both in Catholic Europe and in Asia it is not possible to travel far without coming upon sites invested in this way with a special holiness. The objects which draw men to peregrinate may be divided into three classes: natural features which are in themselves remarkable; places difficult of access, which can only be reached at cost of risk and effort; and sites which have been rendered holy by the visitation of God or the preservation of sacred relics. But this classification is not always clearly defined; for the same object of pilgrimage often falls into two categories at once.

Of striking natural features—self-created objects of veneration, as the Hindus call them—many kinds are found. There are chasms from which issue mysterious vapours, stimulating prophecy, such as Delphi, or Jwala Mukhi, sacred to Hindus and Sikhs, or the Grotta del Cane, near Naples. Caves with their dreadful gloom inspire a sense of supernatural presence. Such are the cave of Trophonius in Boeotia, St. Patrick's cave in Ireland, the grotto of Lourdes, Mariastein near Basle, and the great fissure of Amarnath in Kashmir, with its icy stalactite which is the special object of worship. Some of these add to their sanctity by difficulty of access: St. Patrick's cave is on an island in Lough Derg; Mariastein lies over the edge of a steep cliff; Amarnath is hidden among lofty mountains at 17000 feet above the sea.

Enormous stones, too, are apt to acquire holiness, arousing interest by their vast mass; as though they could hardly have been brought into independent existence, detached from the great earth, without some direct intervention of divine power. Such are the stone at Delphi, or the great rock, now enshrined in a Muhammadan mosque, which no doubt caused men to go up to Jerusalem in Jebusite days, before Israel came out of Egypt. (It is thought by pious Muhammadans to rest in the air without support; their tradition being that at the time of Muhammad's ascension into heaven this stone, which was his point of departure, sought to accompany him but was detained by an angel. To the Hebrews it was sacred as the rock on which Abraham was ready to offer Isaac; and also as a stone which kept down within the earth the receded waters of the Flood.) Meteoric stones have a sanctity as having fallen from heaven: for example, the *lingam* of Jagannath at Puri, and the famous black stone at Mecca.

Wells also, for obvious reasons, tend to attract worship.

Of places inaccessible to which pilgrims toil, some are the sources of rivers, like Gangotri, whence springs the Ganges: others are islands, such as the Îles de Lérins off Cannes, Iona and Lindisfarne, or many off the West coast of Ireland: or distant headlands, like the Spanish Finisterre, or Rameshwaram, the extreme southern cape of the Indian peninsula. More numerous are those which lie high up on mountains or above precipitous rocks; such as the many peaks of Sinai, the lake on Haramuk in Kashmir, the cliffs of Rocamadour in Central France, which Piers Plowman mentions,[1] or the grey cone of Athos. In a mild form such places may frequently be seen, in the pilgrimage churches and chapels which crown modest eminences beside many villages and towns of Catholic Europe: akin no doubt to the high places and hill-altars where lingered the heathen worship that the Israelite priests and prophets were continually trying to exterminate.

The third class of pilgrimage sites is of those which are sanctified through association with divinities or saints or relics: Gaya in Bihar, with its pilgrims' way leading pious Buddhists by long flights of steps up and down the circle of hills, like the great way at Bologna; Jerusalem, Rome,

[1] Right so, if thou be religious, renne thou never ferthere
To Rome ne to Roquemadoure: but as thy rule techeth,
Holde thee to thine obedience: that heighway is to heaven.

Canterbury, Trèves; and Santiago (St. James) de Compostella, rendered attractive also by remote distance. Or a settlement of hermits in a wilderness might become a place of pilgrimage, especially when death had heightened the fame enjoyed during their lives: such as Gueremeh in Cappadocia, St. Bertrand among the Pyrenees, or Einsiedeln above the Lake of Lucerne, where in 1487 died Nicholas the Hermit, reputed to have lived for twenty years without food. And we may make a special category for sacred houses; the Bait-ullah or Qaabah at Mecca, the house of the Virgin at Loretto, St. Columba's at Glencolumbkill, and the house in which St. Francis died, in dei Angeli at Assisi.

In many cases there is definite evidence to show that pilgrimage sites remain sacred even when religions change. Mecca was a resort of pilgrims in the first century B.C., 700 years before Muhammad. The Central-Asian shrines visited by Buddhist pilgrims from China on their way to India, Fa-hsien in the fifth and Hsuan-tsang in the seventh century, are now appropriated to Islam. The so-called footmark on Adam's Peak in Ceylon has been attributed by Brahmans to Siva, by Buddhists to Sakyamuni, by Gnostics to Ieu, by Muhammadans to Adam, and by the Portuguese Christians to either St. Thomas or the eunuch of Candace, queen of Ethiopia.[1]

In the age we are considering, we hear of Henry VII,

[1] J. E. Tennent's *Ceylon* (1860), ii. 133, quoted in Yule's *Marco Polo*, ed. H. Cordier, 1903, ii. 321.

Henry VIII, and even Wolsey going as pilgrims to Our Lady of Walsingham in Norfolk; and Colet took Erasmus with him to Canterbury. But the most renowned places of Christian pilgrimage were Rome, Santiago, and Jerusalem. Thither journeyed pilgrims in great numbers from all parts of Europe; bishops and abbots and clergy, both regular and secular, noblemen of every degree, wealthy merchants, scholars from the universities, civil officials and courtiers, and occasionally even women. Piety or superstition were doubtless the usual motives which led men to face the very considerable perils of the journey; but besides this there was probably in some cases the desire to see new scenes, and a love of adventure for its own sake. Holiday travel was scarcely known in those days. The discomforts were great, and there were still dangers of the ordinary kind, even in the most settled parts of Europe. The beginning of a story in one of More's English works shows how such travel was regarded—as at least unwise, and perhaps extravagant: 'Now was there a young gentleman which had married a merchant's wife. And having a little wanton money which him thought burned out the bottom of his purse, in the first year of his wedding he took his wife with him and went over the sea, for none other errand but to see Flanders and France, and ride out one summer in those countries.' But in the company of pilgrims there was some security, and accordingly the adventurous availed themselves of such opportunities. Thus Peter Falk, burgomaster of Freiburg in Switzerland, went on pilgrimage to Jerusalem in 1515 and again in 1519; and had he not died on the second journey, he was projecting a visit to Portugal and Spain, perhaps to Compostella. He was a keen, interested man. A companion, who was a Cambridge scholar, describes him as taking an ape with him on board to make fun for his shipmates; wearing a gun hanging at his belt, being curious in novelties; carefully noting the names of places and the situations of towns, and using red ink to mark his guide-book.

The literature of pilgrimages is abundant, and consists primarily in narratives written by pilgrims themselves. A few of these were printed by the writers in their own day; many have been published by antiquarians in isolated periodicals; and in the volumes of the Palestine Pilgrims' Text Society there is a collection of translations. Professor Röhricht of Innsbruck has made a wonderful bibliography of German pilgrims to the Holy Land, replete with information and references. The narratives necessarily traverse the same ground, and repeat one another in many points; often reproducing from an early source exactly identical information of the guide-book order as to sites, routes, preparations, precautions, and so forth.

We have three English narratives of Erasmus' period: by William Wey, Fellow of Eton, who went to Jerusalem in 1458 and again in 1462; by Sir Richard Guilford, a Court official who made the journey in 1506; and by Sir Richard Torkington, a parish priest from Norfolk, who went in 1517. But besides these some Baedekers of the time survive; one entitled 'Information for Pilgrims unto the Holy Land',[1] which was printed by Wynkyn de Worde at Westminster in 1498, and again by him in London in 1515 and 1524; another written by Hermann Kunig of Vach in 1495 and several times printed before 1521, 'Die Walfart vnd Strass zu sant Jacob',[2] which gives the distance of each stage and notes inns and hospitals at which shelter might be found.

The Compostella pilgrimage was popular for many reasons, and no doubt began long before St. James had ousted St. Vincent from being patron-saint of Spain. The spot was remote, literally then at the end of the earth, 'beyond which', as another pilgrim says, 'there is no land any more, only water'. There was a great stone, too, in which later piety found the boat that had borne the saint's body from Jerusalem. And there were islands to be visited, one a St. Michael's Mount, round the shores of which should be gathered the cockle shells that were the emblems of pilgrimage duly performed: though the less active bought them at stalls high-heaped outside the cathedral doors, and the rich had them copied in silver and gold.

To the 'end of the earth' Northern Europe went

[1] It has been reproduced with an introduction by Mr. E. G. Duff, London, 1893.

[2] It has been reproduced with an introduction by Professor K. Häbler, Strasburg, 1899.

most easily by sea, all others by land. Convoys gathered in Dartmouth in the lengthening days of spring, and crept along Slapton sands and round the unlighted Start, until there was no land any more, and summoning their courage they must steer out into the Bay of Biscay. This way went John of Gaunt to St. James in 1386, to be crowned King of Castile in the great Romanesque cathedral; and so, too, Chaucer must have pictured the Wyf of Bath visiting 'Galice'.

But Kunig's route lay overland: from Einsiedeln to Romans and Valence; over the Rhone by the famed bridge of the Holy Spirit, which even kings must cross on foot, to Uzès, Nîmes and Béziers; and then westwards into the sandy scant-populated lands where the track was scarcely to be found, except for the pilgrims' graves, often nameless, sometimes perhaps marked with such simple inscriptions as may still be seen on trees and crosses among the forests of the Alps. A Pyrenean pass led him to Roncesvalles; at Logroño the ancient bridge brought him over the Ebro, and so by Burgos and Leon to his journey's end, blessing the patrons—Kings of France and England and Navarre, Dukes of Burgundy—who had raised shelters for poor pilgrims on the way, and above all the Catholic Kings whose munificence had built a huge serai to welcome them in Santiago itself.

For Jerusalem the usual point of departure was Venice. Pilgrims congregated there from all parts of Western and Central Europe, and there were regular services of ships, sailing mostly in the summer months. The competition between shipmasters, or 'patrons', to secure custom was very keen. Thus Torkington records: 'On 3 May the patron of a new goodly ship with other merchants desired us pilgrims that we would come aboard and see his ship within: which ship lay afore St. Mark's Church. We all went in, and there they made us goodly cheer with diverse subtilties, as comfits and marchpanes and sweet wines. Also 5 May the patron of another ship which lay in the sea five miles from Venice, desired us all pilgrims that we would come and see his ship. And the same day we all went with him; and there he provided for us a marvellous good dinner, where we had all manner of good victuals and wine.' Ultimately, Torkington sailed in a new ship of 800 tons,[1] under a patron named Thomas Dodo. Only three days later another ship set sail with a large party of German pilgrims.

In all ages a great ship is a great wonder, representing for the time the final triumph of the shipwright's art. The monster vessel that set Lucian's friend dreaming at the Piraeus had but one mast; yet the curious from Athens flocked down to see her extraordinary proportions and to admire the sailors who had beaten up in her from Egypt against the Etesian winds in only seventy days. She was

[1] If the figure is correct, she was a large vessel for the times; for a century later, the *Pelican*, in which Drake sailed round the world, was only 100 tons, the *Squirrel*, in which Sir Humfrey Gilbert was cast away in an Atlantic gale, only 10.

the ship of the hour: anything greater scarcely conceivable. Again, Macaulay returning from India in 1837 compares his comfortable sailing-ship to a huge floating hotel. Burton on his way to Mecca in 1853, when steaming across the Bay of Biscay in a vessel of 2000 tons, prophesies that sea-sickness is at an end now that such monsters ply across the ocean and laugh at the storm. How puny do they seem beside the Olympic and Imperator, at which we in our turn gaze wonderingly and think that engineering can no further go. It is amusing to find the same proud admiration in a traveller of 1517: 'Our ship was so great that when we came to land, we could not run her upon the beach like a galley, but must remain in deep water', the passengers going ashore in boats.

Quite a number of contracts between patron and pilgrim have been preserved. Some of the terms are as follows: 'that the ship shall be properly armed and manned, and carry a barber and a physician; that it shall only touch at the usual ports, and not stay more than three days at Cyprus, because of malaria there.' The Holy Land was in Turkish hands, and the Turks, though willing to receive the pilgrims, for the sake of the money they brought into the country, were not sorry to have opportunities of teaching the 'Christian dogs' their place. The authorities maintained some semblance of order and justice, but took little trouble to control their underlings; and in consequence the pilgrims suffered all kinds of minor oppressions. It is not surprising therefore to find that the contract stipulated that the patron should accompany them on all their journeyings in the Holy Land, even as far as the Jordan, and that he should pay all the tolls and tributes for them, except the small tips, just as Cook does to-day, and also make all arrangements for such pilgrims as wished to go on to Sinai. In view of this last possibility the stipulation was sometimes made that only half the passage-money should be paid at Venice; the other half at Jaffa on the return-journey. If a pilgrim died on the journey, the patron might not bury him at sea, unless there was no immediate prospect of reaching land.

The voyage outwards could be done in a month, but often took longer if the weather was bad, or if long halts were made at Rhodes and Cyprus. On shore the pilgrims worked as hard as any 'conducted' party to-day, being herded about to one sacred site after another, to the Holy Sepulchre, the vale of Josaphat, the Mount of Olives, Bethlehem, the mountains of Judea, the Jordan, and receiving in each place 'clean absolution'. Twelve or thirteen days was a fair time to allow for all this, including one or two days each way between Jaffa and Jerusalem; but Guilford's party were given 22. On the other hand we hear of another company which did it in nine.

The Holy Land guide-book of which we spoke is full of practical advice of all sorts: about distances, rates of exchange, terms of contract with a shipmaster, tributes to be paid to the Saracens, and finally vocabularies of useful words, in Moresco, Greek, Turkish. Here are a few specimens:

'If ye shall go in a galley, make your covenant with the patron betime; and choose you a place in the said galley in the overmost stage. For in the lowest under it is right evil and smouldering hot and stinking.' The fare in this to Jaffa and back from Venice, including food, was 50 ducats, 'for to be in a good honest place, and to have your ease in the galley and also to be cherished'. In a carrick the fare was only 30 ducats: there 'choose you a chamber as nigh the middes of the ship as ye may; for there is least rolling or tumbling, to keep your brain and stomach in temper'. Amongst other arrangements to be made with the patron, 'Covenant that ye come not at Famagust in Cyprus for no thing. For many Englishmen and other also have died. For that air is so corrupt there about, and the water there also. Also see that the said patron give you every day hot meat twice at two meals, the forenoon at dinner and the afternoon at supper. And that the wine that ye shall drink be good, and the water fresh and not stinking, if ye come to have better, and also the biscuit.'

The traveller is recommended to buy in Venice a padlock with which to keep his cabin locked, three barrels, two for wine and one for water, and a chest to hold his stores and things: 'For though ye shall be at table with the patron, yet notwithstanding, ye shall full ofttimes have need to your own victuals, as bread, cheese, eggs, wine and other to make your collation. For some time ye shall have feeble bread and feeble wine and stinking water, so that many times ye will be right fain to eat of your own.' Besides this he will want 'confections and confortatives, green ginger, almonds, rice, figs, raisins great and small, pepper, saffron, cloves and loaf sugar'. For equipment he should take 'a little caldron, a frying-pan, dishes, plates, saucers, cups of glass, a grater for bread and such necessaries'. 'Also ye shall buy you a bed beside St. Mark's Church in Venice, where ye shall have a feather-bed, a mattress, a pillow, two pair sheets and a quilt' for three ducats. 'And when ye come again, bring the same bed again, and ye shall have a ducat and a half for it again, though it be broken and worn. And mark his house and his name that ye bought it of, against ye come to Venice.' Further needs are 'a cage for half a dozen of hens or chickens' and 'half a bushel of millet seed for them': also 'a barrel for a siege for your chamber in the ship. It is full necessary, if ye were sick, that ye come not in the air.' The malady here considered is probably not that which is usually associated with the sea; though pilgrims were not immune from this any more than from other troubles.

On coming to haven towns, 'if ye shall tarry there three days, go betimes to land, for then ye may have lodging before another; for it will be taken up anon'. Similarly at Jaffa in choosing a mount for the ride up to Jerusalem 'be not too long behind your fellows; for an ye come betime, ye may choose the best mule' and 'ye shall pay no more for the best than for the worst'. 'Also take good heed to your knives and other small japes that ye bear upon you: for the Saracens will go talking by you and make good cheer; but they will steal from you if they may.' 'Also when ye shall ride to flume Jordan, take with you out of Jerusalem bread, wine, water, hard eggs and cheese and such victuals as ye may have for two days. For by all that way there is none to sell.'

Let us turn now to an individual narrative,[1] that of Felix Fabri, a learned and sensible Dominican of Ulm (1442–1502). He had already made the journey once, out of piety, in 1480, with the company mentioned above, which had only nine days on shore. He was desirous to go also to St. Catherine's at Mount Sinai because she was his patroness-saint, to whom he had devoted himself on entering the Dominican order on her day (25 November) in 1452; and accordingly for the second time, in 1483, he procured from the Pope the permission, which every one needed, to visit the Holy Land: those that went without this being ipso facto excommunicate, until they did penance before the Warden of the Franciscans at Jerusalem. He gives us a picture of all that he went through, in the most minute details. During the day we see the pilgrims crowded together on deck, some drinking and singing, others playing dice or cards or that unfailing pastime for ship-life,

[1] It has been translated by Mr. Aubrey Stewart for the Palestine Pilgrims' Text Society, vols. 7–10, 1892–3.

chess. Talking, reading, telling their beads, writing diaries, sleeping, hunting in their clothes for vermin ; so they spend their day. Some for exercise climb up the rigging, or jump, or brandish heavy weights : some drift about from one party to another, just watching what is going on. Our good friar complains of the habits of the noblemen, who gambled a great deal and were always making small wagers, which they paid with a cup of Malmsey wine. He also tells how the patron, to beguile the journey, produced a great piece of silk, which he offered as a prize for the pilgrims to play for.

At meal times, to which they are summoned by trumpets, the pilgrims race on to the poop : for they cannot all find seats, and those that come late have to sit among the crew. Noblemen, who have their own servants, are too fastidious to mingle with the crowd ; and pay extra to the cooks,—poor, sweating fellows, toiling crossly in a tiny galley—for food which their servants bring to them on the main-deck, or even below. After the pilgrims, the captain and his council dine in state off silver dishes ; and the captain's wine is tasted before he drinks it. At night all sleep below, in a cabin the dirt of which is indescribable. They wrangle over the places where they shall spread their beds, and knives are drawn. Some obstinately keep their candles burning, even though missiles come flying. Others talk noisily ; and the drunken, even when quiet, snore. No wonder the poor friar longed for the peace of his own cell at home in Ulm.

Fabri has much practical advice to give. He bids his reader be careful in going up and down the companion, veritably a ladder in those times; not to sit down upon ropes, or on places covered with pitch, which often melts in the sun; not to get in the way of the crew and make them angry; not to drop things overboard or let his hat be blown off. 'Let the pilgrim beware of carrying a light upon deck at night; for the mariners dislike this strangely, and cannot endure lights when they are at work.' Small things are apt to be stolen, if left about: for on board ship men have no other way to get what they want. 'While you are writing, if you lay down your pen and turn your face away, your pen will be lost, even though you be among men whom you know: and if you lose it, you will have exceeding great trouble in getting another.'

To Fabri's annoyance the ship's company included one woman, an elderly lady, who came on board at the last moment with her husband, a Fleming. 'She seemed,' he says, 'when we first saw her, to be restless and inquisitive; as indeed she was. She ran hither and thither incessantly about the ship, and was full of curiosity, wanting to hear and see everything, and made herself hated exceedingly. Her husband was a decent man, and for his sake many held their tongues; but had he not been there, it would have gone hard with her. This woman was a thorn in the eyes of us all.' His delight was great, when she was left behind at Rhodes, having strayed away to some church outside the town. 'Except her husband, no one was sorry.' But their peace was short-lived, for this active lady procured a boat and overtook them at Cyprus; and Fabri could not help pitying the straits she had been put to. We may rather admire her courage in undertaking the pilgrimage at all, and especially the resource which she displayed on this very unpleasant emergency.

On the eve of St. John Baptist, after dark, the sailors made St. John's fire; stringing forty horn lanterns on a rope to the maintop, amid shouts and trumpeting and clapping of hands. Upon which Fabri makes this curious remark: 'Before this I never had beheld the practice of clapping the hands for joy, as it is said in Psalm 46. Nor could I have believed that the general clapping of many men's hands would have such great power to move the human mind to rejoicing.' With some misgiving he goes on to record that after the festivity the ship was left to drive of itself, both pilgrims and sailors betaking themselves to rest.

At Cyprus they had a few days, and Fabri led some of his companions to the summit of Mount Stavrovuni, near their port Salinae (Citium by the salt lakes of Larnaka), to visit the Church of Holy Cross—the cross of Dismas, the thief on the right hand, said to have been brought by that great finder of relics, the Empress Helena. By the way he was careful to explain that they must expect no miracle: 'we shall see none in Jerusalem, so how can there be one here?' In the church he read them a mass and preached, and at departing rang the church bell, saying that they would hear no bells again till they returned to Christendom.

When they set sail again, all eyes were turned Eastwards: happy would he be who should first sight the land of their desire. Fabri crept forward to the prow of the galley and sat for hours upon the horns, straining his gaze across the summer seas which whispered around the ship's stem: almost, he confesses, cursing night when it fell and cut off all hope till dawn. Before sunrise he was there again, and on 1 July the watchman in the maintop gave the glad shout. The pilgrims flocked up on deck and sang Te Deum with bounding joy. It was a tumult of harsh voices; but to Fabri in his happiness their various dissonance made sweet harmony.

On reaching Jaffa they lay for some days awaiting permission to land. At length all was ready. The ship's officers collected the tips due to them, and the pilgrims were put on shore: falling to kiss the ground as they struggled out of their boats through the surf. One by one they were brought before Turkish officials, who took record of their names and their fathers' names—an occasion on which noblemen often tried to pass themselves off as of low degree, to escape the higher fees due. Fabri notes that his Christian name, Felix, gave the official recorders some trouble: that he pronounced it again and again for them, but they could get nothing at all like it. Each pilgrim, when entered, was hurried off by Saracens, like sheep into a pen, and thrust into a row of caves along the sea-shore, known as St. Peter's

Cellars. If they had suffered on board ship, their sufferings were multiplied now tenfold. Strict watch was kept upon them, and no one was allowed to leave the caves. Within, the ground was covered with semi-liquid filth. From the ship, as they lay waiting to land, Fabri had noticed the Saracens running in and out of the caves ; and he argued that they were intentionally defiling them, to make it more disagreeable to the Christian dogs. But this seems hardly necessary. There had doubtless been other pilgrims before them. Droves of mankind can tread ground into a foul swamp as cattle tread a farmyard. With their feet the poor pilgrims managed to collect some of the impurities together into a heap in the centre ; each man clearing enough space to lie down upon. Fabri found solace to his offended senses in thinking of his dear Lord lying in a hard manger, amongst all the defilements of the oxen.

After a time came traders selling rushes and branches of trees to make beds, unguents and perfumes and frankincense to burn, and attar of roses from Damascus. Others brought bread and water and lettuces and hot cakes made with eggs, which the pilgrims gladly bought ; and, as the day wore on, with the much going to and fro the ground was slowly dried under their feet. At nightfall appeared a man armed, whom they took to be the owner of the caves. With menaces he extorted from each of them a penny, and in the morning again, before they could come out, another penny ; to their great indignation against the captains and dragoman, who were sleeping in tents higher up the hill, and had by contract undertaken all these charges. So long as they were there, the pilgrims suffered continual annoyance from the Turks, who ran in among them pilfering, breaking any wine bottles they found, and provoking them to blows, in order to secure the fines of which the pilgrims would then be mulcted. One young man was so disgusted at it all that he went back on board and gave up his pilgrimage; living with the crew till the party came back from Jerusalem. They were indeed entirely in the hands of the Turks. It was not a case of moving when they were inclined. When the Turks wished, they were allowed to go forward: till then they were confined like prisoners. No date was fixed: the pilgrims just had to wait in patience, hoping that tomorrow or tomorrow or tomorrow would see them start.

Fabri records, however, that there was some justice available. Petty wrongs must go unredressed; but a pilgrim who had been gulled into buying coloured glass as gems to the value of five ducats, recovered his money by complaining to the local governor. A subordinate came down, took the money from the fraudulent trader by force, and restored it to its owner. Again Fabri testifies to the careful way in which the escort protected the company from molestation on its way up to Jerusalem. He is also at pains to refute the idea that the Turks compelled them to ride on donkeys, lest the land should be defiled by Christian feet: rather, he says, it is for our comfort and convenience. And indeed there was sufficient refutation in the regulation which compelled them to dismount on reaching any village and proceed through its narrow streets on foot.

Whilst waiting at Jaffa, Fabri to his great delight fell in with the donkey-boy who had gone up with him three years before; and was able to secure him again. The boy welcomed him, especially as Fabri had brought him a present of two iron stirrups from Ulm; and all the way served him most faithfully, picking him figs and grapes from the gardens they passed, sharing water and biscuit, and even giving him a goad for his mount—a concession which was not allowed to the ordinary pilgrim.

Their first march was to Ramlah, and on arrival they were penned for the day into a great serai, built by a Duke of Burgundy. It was still early, only 9 o'clock, for they had started before sunrise. After barring the gate to keep out the Turks, they set up an altar and celebrated mass. A sermon was preached by the Franciscan Warden of Jerusalem, in the course of which he gave them advice as to their behaviour towards those to whose tolerance they owed their position there—counsels which forty years later the fiery spirit of Loyola burned to set at nought, till the Franciscans were thankful to get him safely out of Jerusalem without open flouting of the masters—: not to go about alone; not to enter mosques or step over graves; not to insult Saracens when at prayer or by touching their beards; not to return blow for blow, but to make formal complaints; not to drink wine openly; to observe decorum and not rush to be first at the sacred sites; and generally to be circumspect in presence of the infidels, lest they mark what was done amiss and say, 'O thou bad Christian', a phrase which was familiar to them in both Italian and German. He further charged them that they must on no account chip fragments off the Holy Sepulchre and other sacred buildings; nor write their names or coats of arms upon the walls; and finally, he advised them to be careful in any money-transactions with Muhammadans, and to have no dealings at all with either Eastern Christians or German Jews.

After mass was over, they opened the gate and found the outer court filled with traders who brought them excellent food: fowls ready roasted, puddings of rice and milk, capital bread and eggs, and fruit of every kind, grapes, pomegranates, apples, oranges (pomerancia), lemons and water-melons; and in the afternoon they were allowed to go and have hot baths in the splendid marble hamáms. In the evening came a rumour that they were to proceed. They packed up their bundles and sat waiting for an hour or two; and then the rumour proved to be false. Meanwhile the sleeping-mats which they had hired for their stay had been rolled up by their owners and carried off; and the pilgrims had to sleep as best they might. Fabri made his way up on to the roof and passed the night there.

Waking early before sunrise he was much impressed

to observe the devotion of the Muhammadans at their morning prayers: the long rows of kneeling figures, swaying forward together in reverent prostration, the grave faces and solemn tones. Surely, as he looked, he must have felt that God, even his God, was the God of all the earth, and would be a Father to those that sought Him so earnestly. At any rate he turned away, with a strong sense of contrast, to his own comrades waking to the day with laughing chatter and no thought of prayer. An episode of this halt was a visit from a Saracen fruit-seller upon whom Fabri looked with curiosity. Then, taking the man's hat, he spat upon it with every expression of disgust at its Saracen badge. The man, instead of resenting it, looked cautiously round and then spat on the badge himself, at the same time making the sign of the Cross. He was a Christian who had been forced into conversion, probably in expiation of some crime; and now hated his life. It was no uncommon thing. As their procession wound through village streets, the pilgrims would often see furtive signs made to them from inner chambers: unwilling converts signalling the symbol that they loved, to eyes that were sure to be sympathetic.

As Fabri made his way along, his heart was glad. His foot was on holy ground, and at every step new associations came floating into his thoughts. These were the mountains to which Moses had looked from Pisgah; here Jephthah's daughter had made plaint for her young life; hither had come Mary in the joy of the angel's message; the stones on which he stumbled might have felt the feet of Christ. At the hill called Mount Joy they should have seen Jerusalem; but the air was thick, and they could only make out the Mount of Olives. So they toiled on along their dusty way, between dry stone walls and thirsty vegetable-gardens, until, as they reached the crest of a low ridge, suddenly like a flash of light it shone before them, the City, the Holy City.

At once their footsteps quickened with new life; and when at length they found themselves in the courtyard of the Church of the Holy Sepulchre, their pent-up emotions burst forth, into tears and groans, sweet wailings and deep sighs. Some lay powerless on the ground, forsaken by their strength and to all appearances dead. Others drifted from one corner to another, beating their breasts, as though urged by an evil spirit. Some knelt bare-kneed; as they prayed, stretching out their arms like a rood. Others were shaken with such violent sobs that they could only sit down and hold their heads in their hands. Some lost all command of themselves, and, forgetting how to behave, sought to please God with strange and childish gestures. On the other hand, Fabri noted some who stood quite unmoved, and merely mocked at the strange display: dull, unprofitable souls he calls them, brute beasts, not having the spirit of God. Their self-contained temperament misliked him, especially as thereafter they held aloof from those who had given way to such enthusiasm or, as they felt it, weakness.

We cannot company with the party to all the numerous sites that piety bade them visit. It was prodigiously fatiguing for them under the July sun, and the ranks grew thin as the weaker spirits fell out dead tired, to rest awhile in hospitable cloister or by cooling well. Fabri found it very toilsome to struggle after mental abstraction, to rise to such heights as he desired of devotion and comprehension of all the holy influences around him, to seize every opportunity of contemplation and lose nothing; being soon thoroughly exhausted with his bodily exertions. Some alleviation there was: when holy women—nuns of his own Order, who had a house in Jerusalem—washed his scapular and tunic for him, and wrought other works of charity for which he was very grateful.

The pilgrims had been warned not to wander away from their party. One day as they went to the Dead Sea, they halted at a monastery; and Fabri was tempted to ramble off alone to inspect a cliff which had been hollowed out by hermits into innumerable caves. It was a precipitous place; and at one point, where the path was narrow and the cliff fell sheer below, he encountered an Eastern Christian. Seeing that Fabri was afraid, the fellow began to trifle with him and demanded money; and in the end Fabri was obliged to open his slender purse. 'Ever since then', he says, 'I have abhorred the company of Christians of that sort more than that of Saracens and Arabs, and have trusted them less. Though perhaps he would not have thrown me down the precipice, even had I given him nothing, yet it was wicked of him to play with me in a place of such danger. If an Arab had done so, I should have been pleased at his play, and should have held him to be a good pagan; but I believe no good of that Christian.' When he rejoined his party, the patron told him that the Eastern Christians were least to be trusted of any men.

On arrival at Jordan there was much excitement. To bathe in that ancient river was thought to renew youth, and so all the pilgrims were eager to immerse themselves; even women of 80—a rather doubtful figure—plunging into the lukewarm stream. Some had brought bells to be blessed with Jordan water, others strips of material for clothes; and wealthier members of the party jumped in as they were, in order that the robes they had on might bring them luck in the future. Three things were forbidden to the pilgrims: (1) to swim across the stream, because in the excitement of emotion and amongst such crowds individuals had often been drowned; (2) to dive in, because the bottom was muddy; (3) to carry away phials of Jordan water. The first regulation was openly violated. On his first journey Fabri had swum across, but on the return had been seized with panic and nearly drowned. So this time he contented himself with drawing up his garments round his neck and sitting down in the shallow water among the crowd who were splashing about and jestingly baptizing one another. The prohibition of Jordan water was to appease the shipmen; for it was thought to cause storms when carried over the sea.

We have not time to follow Fabri in more detail. On 24 August he left Jerusalem with a small company of pilgrims who had not been deterred from undertaking the journey to Sinai. There was much dispute about the route they should follow. Some were for going by sea to Alexandria, others wished to march down the sea coast; but finally they made up their minds to go straight South across the desert. Starting from Gaza on 9 September they reached St. Catherine's on the 22nd. Five days of very hard work sufficed for them to see all the sacred sites and ascend the many towering peaks; and here again Fabri impressed upon his companions that the days of miracles were over, and that in these evil times God would show no more. On 27 September they set forth again, and journeying through Midian reached Cairo on 8 October; having picked up on the shore of the Red Sea oyster shells which should be an abiding witness of their pilgrimage. On 5 November they set sail from Alexandria; but summer had departed from the sea, and the winds blew obstinately. Three times they beat up to Cape Malea, before they could round the point and make sail for the North; and it was not till 8 Jan. 1484 that they landed in Venice. The pilgrimage was over after seven months, and with what Guilford's chaplain calls 'large departing of our money'.

X

THE TRANSALPINE RENAISSANCE

HITHERTO we have viewed the age mainly through the personality of individuals. It remains to consider some of the features of the Renaissance when it had spread across the Alps—to France, to Spain, to Switzerland, to Germany, to England—and some of the contrasts that it presents with the earlier movement in Italy. The story of the Italian Renaissance has often been told; and we need not go back upon it here. On the side of the revival of learning it was without doubt the great age. The importance of its discoveries, the fervour of its enthusiasm have never been equalled. But though it remains pre-eminent, the period that followed it has an interest of its own which is hardly less keen and presents the real issues at stake in a clearer light. Awakened Italy felt itself the heiress of Rome, and thus patriotism coloured its enthusiasm for the past. To the rest of Western Europe this source of inspiration was not open. They were compelled to examine more closely the aims before them; and thus attained to a calmer and truer estimate of what they might hope to gain from the study of the classics. It was not the revival of lost glories, thoughts of a world held in the bonds of peace: in those dreams the Transalpines had only the part of the conquered. Rather the classics led them back to an age before Christianity; and pious souls though they were, the scholar's instinct told them that they would find there something to learn. Christianity had fixed men's eyes on the future, on their own salvation in the life to come; and had trained all knowledge, even Aristotle, to serve that end. In the great days of Greece and Rome the world was free from this absorbing preoccupation; and inquiring spirits were at liberty to find such truth as they could, not merely the truth that they wished or must.

Another point of difference between Italy and the Transalpines is in the resistance offered to the Renaissance in the two regions. The scholastic philosophy and theology was a creation of the North. The greatest of the Schoolmen found their birth or training in France or Germany, at the schools of Paris and Cologne; and with the names of Duns, Hales, Holcot, Occam, Burley and Bradwardine our own islands stand well to the fore. The situation is thus described by Aldus in a letter written to the young prince of Carpi in October 1499, to rejoice over some translations from the Greek just arrived from Linacre in England: 'Of old it was barbarous learning that came to us from Britain; it conquered Italy and still holds our castles. But now they send us learned eloquence; with British aid we shall chase away barbarity and come by our own again.' The teaching of the Schoolmen made its way into Italy, but had little vogue; and with the Church, through such Popes as Nicholas v, on the side of the Renaissance, resistance almost disappeared. The humanists charging headlong dissipated their foes in a moment, but were soon carried beyond the field of battle, to fall into the hands of the forces of reaction. Across the Alps, on the other hand, the Church and the universities stood together and looked askance at the new movement, dreading what it might bring forth. In consequence the ground was only won by slow and painful efforts, but each advance, as it was made, was secured.

The position may be further illustrated by comparing the first productions of the press on either side of the Alps: in the early days, before the export trade had developed, and when books were produced mainly for the home market. The Germans who brought the art down into Italy, Sweynheym and Pannartz at Rome, Wendelin and Jenson at Venice, printed scarcely anything that was not classical: Latin authors and Latin translations from the Greek. Up in the North the first printers of Germany, Fust and Schoeffer at Mainz, Mentelin at Strasburg, rarely overstepped the boundaries of the mediaeval world that was passing away or the modern that was taking its place.

The appearance of the *Epistolae Obscurorum Virorum* in 1515 exposed the scholastic teachers and their allies in the Church to such widespread ridicule that it is not easy for us now to realize the position which those dignitaries still held when

Erasmus was young. The stream of contempt poured upon them by the triumphant humanists obscures the merit of their system as a gigantic and complete engine of thought. Under its great masters, Albert the Great, Thomas Aquinas, Duns Scotus, scholasticism had been rounded into an instrument capable of comprehending all knowledge and of expressing every refinement of thought; and, as has been well said, the acute minds that created it, if only they had extended their inquiries into natural science, might easily have anticipated by centuries the discoveries of modern days.[1] In expressing their distinctions the Schoolmen had thrown to the winds the restraints of classical Latin and the care of elegance; and with many of them language had degenerated into jargon. But in their own eyes their position was unassailable. Their philosophy was founded on Aristotle; and while they were proud of their master, they were prouder still of the system they had created in his name: and thus they felt no impulse to look backwards to the past.

In the matter of language they had been led by a spirit of reaction. The literature of later classical times had sacrificed matter to form; and the schools had been dominated by teachers who trained boys to declaim in elegant periods on any subject whatever, regardless of its content; thus carrying to an extreme the precepts with which the great orators had enforced the importance of style. The Schoolmen swung the pendulum back, letting sound and froth

[1] Cf. F. G. Stokes, *Epistolae Obscurorum Virorum*, 1909, p. xvii.

go and thinking only of their subject-matter, despising the classics. In their turn they were confronted by the humanists, who reasserted the claims of form.

There was sense in the humanist contention. It is very easy to say the right thing in the wrong way; in other spheres than diplomacy the choice of language is important. Words have a history of their own, and often acquire associations independent of their meaning. Rhythm, too, and clearness need attention. An unbalanced sentence goes haltingly and jars; an ambiguous pronoun causes the reader to stumble. An ill-written book, an ill-worded speech fail of their effects; it is not merely by sympathy and character that men persuade. But of course the humanists pushed the matter too far. Pendulums do not reach the repose of the mean without many tos and fros. Elegance is good, but the art of reasoning is not to be neglected. Of the length to which they went Ascham's method of instruction in the *Scholemaster* (1570) is a good example. He wished his scholar to translate Cicero into English, and then from the English to translate back into the actual words of the Latin. The Ciceronians did not believe that the same thing could be well said in many ways; rather there was one way which transcended all others, and that Cicero had attained. Erasmus, however, was no Ciceronian; and one of the reasons why he won such a hold upon his own and subsequent generations was that, more than all his contemporaries, he succeeded in establishing a reasonable accord between the claims of form and matter in literature.

In their neglect of the classics the Schoolmen had a powerful ally. For obvious reasons the early and the mediaeval Church felt that much of classical literature was injurious to the minds of the young, and in consequence discouraged the use of it in schools. The classics were allowed to perish, and their place was taken by Christian poets such as Prudentius or Juvencus, by moralizations of Aesop, patchwork compositions known as 'centos' on Scriptural themes, and the like. The scholars, therefore, who went to Italy and came home to the North carrying the new enthusiasm, had strenuous opposition to encounter. The Schoolmen considered them impertinent, the Church counted them immoral. To us who know which way the conflict ended, the savage blows delivered by the humanists seem mere brutality; they lash their fallen foes with what appears inhuman ferocity. But the truth is that the struggle was not finished until well into the sixteenth century. Biel of Tubingen, 'the last of the Schoolmen', lived till 1495. Between 1501 and 1515 a single printer, Wolff of Basle, produced five massive volumes of the *Summae* of mediaeval Doctors. Through the greater part, therefore, of Erasmus' life the upholders of the old systems and ideals, firmly entrenched by virtue of possession, succeeded in maintaining their supremacy in the schools.

Between the two periods of the revival of learning,

the Italian and the Transalpine, a marked line is drawn by the invention of printing, *c.* 1455: when the one movement had run half its course, the other scarcely begun. The achievements of the press in the diffusion of knowledge are often extolled; and some of the resulting good and evil is not hard to see. But the paramount service rendered to learning by the printer's art was that it made possible a standard of critical accuracy which was so much higher than what was known before as to be almost a new creation. When books were manuscripts, laboriously written out one at a time, there could be no security of identity between original and copy; and even when a number of copies were made from the same original, there was a practical certainty that there would be no absolute uniformity among them. Mistakes were bound to occur; not always at the same point, but here in one manuscript, there in another. Or again, when two unrelated copies of the same book were brought together, there was an antecedent probability that examination would reveal differences: so that in general it was impossible to feel that a fellow-scholar working on the same author was using the same text.

Even with writers of one's own day uniformity was hardly to be attained. Not uncommonly, as a mark of attention, an author revised manuscript copies of his works, which were to be presented to friends; and besides correcting the copyists' errors, might add or cut out or alter passages according to his later judgement. Subsequent copies would doubtless follow his revision, and then the process might be repeated; with the result that a reader could not tell to what stage in the evolution of a work the text before him might belong: whether it represented the earliest form of composition or the final form reached perhaps many years afterwards. To understand the conditions under which mediaeval scholars worked, it is of the utmost importance to realize this state of uncertainty and flux.

Not that in manuscript days there was indifference to accuracy. Serious scholars and copyists laid great stress upon it. With insistent fervour they implored one another to be careful, and to collate what had been copied. But there are limits to human powers. Collation is a dull business; and unless done with minute attention, cannot be expected to yield perfect correctness. When a man has copied a work of any length, it is hard for him to collate it with the original slowly. Physically, of course, he easily might: but the spirit is weak, and, weary of the ground already traversed once, urges him to hurry forward, with the inevitable result.

With a manuscript, too, the possible reward might well seem scarcely worth the labour; for how could any permanence be ensured for critical work? A scholar might expend his efforts over a corrupt author, might compare his own manuscript with others far and near, and at length arrive at a text really more correct. And yet what hope had he that his labour was not lost? His manuscript would pass at his death into other hands and might easily be overlooked and even perish. Like a child's castle built upon the sand, his work would be overwhelmed by the rising tide of oblivion. Such conditions are disheartening.

Thus mediaeval standards of accuracy were of necessity low. In default of good instruments we content ourselves with those we have. To draw a line straight we use a ruler; but if one is not to be had, the edge of a book or a table may supply its place. In the last resort we draw roughly by hand, but with no illusions as to our success. So it was with the scholar of the Middle Ages. His instruments were imperfect; and he acquiesced in the best standards he could get: realizing no doubt their defects, but knowing no better way.

But with printing the position was at once changed. When the type had been set up, it was possible to strike off a thousand copies of a book, each of which was identical with all the rest. It became worth while to spend abundant pains over seeking a good text and correcting the proofs—though this latter point was not perceived at first—when there was the assured prospect of such uniformity to follow. One edition could be distinguished from another by the dates on title-page and colophon; and work once done was done for all time, if enough copies of a book were taken off. This necessarily produced a great change in methods of study. Instead of a single manuscript, in places perhaps hopelessly entangled, and always at the mercy of another manuscript of equal or greater authority that might appear from the blue with different readings, the scholar received a text which represented a recension of, it may be, several manuscripts, and whose roughnesses had been smoothed out by the care of editors more or less competent.

The precious volumes to which modern book-lovers reverently give the title of 'Editio princeps', had almost as great honour in their own day, before the credit of priority and antiquity had come to them; for in them men saw the creation of a series of 'standard texts', norms to which, until they were superseded, all future work upon the same ground could be referred. As a result, too, of the improved correctness of the texts, instead of being satisfied with the general sense of an author, men were able to base edifices of precise argument upon the verbal meaning of passages, in some confidence that their structures would not be overset.

But the new invention was not universally acclaimed. Trithemius with his conservative mind quickly detected some weaknesses; and in 1492 he composed a treatise 'In praise of scribes', in vain attempt to arrest the flowing tide. 'Let no one say, "Why should I trouble to write books, when they are appearing continually in such numbers? for a moderate sum one can acquire a large library." What a difference between the results achieved! A manuscript written on parchment will last a thousand years: books printed on paper will scarcely live two hundred. Besides, there will always be something to copy: not everything can be printed. Even if it could, a true scribe ought not to give up. His pen can perpetuate good works which otherwise would soon perish. He must not be amazed by the present abundance that he sees, but should look forward to the needs of the future. Though we had thousands of volumes, we must not cease writing; for printed books are never so good. Indeed they usually pay little heed to ornament and orthography.' It is noticeable that only in this last point does Trithemius claim for manuscripts superior accuracy. In the matter of permanence we may wonder what he would have thought of modern paper.

The first advance, then, rendered possible by the invention of printing was to more uniform and better texts: the next step forward was no less important. To scholars content with the general sense of a work, a translation might be as acceptable as the original. Improved standards of accuracy led men to perceive that an author must be studied in his own tongue: in order that no shade of meaning might be lost. Here again the two periods are easily distinguished. Nicholas V set his scholars, Poggio and Valla, to translate the Greeks, Herodotus and Thucydides, Aristotle and Diodorus. The feature of the later epoch is the number of Greek editions which came out to supplant the versions in common use. The credit for this advance in critical scholarship must be given to Aldus for his Greek Aristotle, which appeared in 1495–9; and he subsequently led the way with numerous texts of the Greek classics. At the same time he proposed to apply the same principle to Biblical study. As early as 1499 Grocin in a letter alludes to Aldus' scheme of printing the whole Bible in the original 'three languages', Hebrew, Greek and Latin; and a specimen was actually put forth in 1501.

In this matter precedence might seem to lie with the Jewish printers, who produced the Psalms in Hebrew in 1477, and the Old Testament complete in 1488; but as the Jews never at any period ceased to read their Scriptures in Hebrew, there was no question of recovery of an original. Aldus did not live to carry his scheme out; and it was left to Ximenes and the band of scholars that he gathered at Alcala, to produce the first edition of the Bible complete in the original tongues, the Complutensian Polyglott, containing the Hebrew side by side with the Septuagint and the Vulgate, and for the Pentateuch a Syriac paraphrase. The New Testament in this great enterprise was finished in 1514, and the whole work was ready by 1517, shortly before Ximenes' death. But as publication was delayed till 1522, the actual priority rests with Erasmus, whose New Testament in Greek with a Latin translation by himself appeared, as we have seen, in 1516.

Thus by an accident Germany gained the credit of being the first to assert this new principle, the importance of studying texts in the original, in the field where resistance is most resolute and victory is hardly won. And now it was about to enter upon a still greater contest. Erasmus' New Testament encountered hostile criticism in many quarters: conservative theologians made common cause with the friars in condemning it. But at the very centre of the religion they professed, the book was blessed by the chief priests. The Pope accepted the dedication, and bishops wished they could read the Greek. Far otherwise was it with the impending struggle of the Reformation: there the cleavage of sides followed very different lines. Into that wide field we cannot now expatiate; but it is important to notice an element which the German Renaissance contributed to the Reformation, and which played a considerable part in both movements—the accentuation of German national feeling.

At the middle of the fifteenth century Italy enjoyed undisputed pre-eminence in the world of learning. The sudden splendour into which the Renaissance had blazed up on Italian soil drew men's eyes thither more than ever; and to its ancient universities students from the North swarmed like bees. To graduate in Italy, to hear its famous doctors, perhaps even to learn from one of the native Greeks brought over out of the East, became first the ambition, and then the indispensable requirement of every Northern scholar who could afford it; and few of Erasmus' friends and colleagues had not at some time or other made the pilgrimage to Italy. Consequence and success brought the usual Nemesis. The Italian *hubris* expressed itself in the familiar Greek distinction between barbarian and home-born; and the many nations from beyond the Alps found themselves united in a common bond which they were not eager to share. We have seen the kind of gibe with which Agricola's eloquence was greeted at Pavia. The more such insults are deserved, the more they sting. We may be sure that in many cases they were not forgotten. Celtis returning from Italy to Ingolstadt in 1492 delivered his soul in an inaugural oration: 'The ancient hatred between us can never be dissolved. But for the Alps we should be eternally at war.' In other countries the feeling, though less acute, was much the same. Thus in 1517 spoke Stephen Poncher, bishop of Paris, after his first meeting with Erasmus: 'Italy has no one to compare with him in literary gifts. In our own day Hermolaus and Politian have rescued Latin from barbarism; and their services can never be forgotten. When I was there, too, I met a number of men of rare ability and learning. But with all respect to the Italians, I must say that Erasmus eclipses every one, Transalpine and Cisalpine alike.'

Of the foreign 'nations' at the universities of Italy none was more numerous than the German, a title which embraced many nationalities of the North: not merely German-speaking races such as the Swiss and Flemish and Dutch, but all who could by any stretch of imagination be represented as descendants of the Goths; Swedes and Danes, Hungarians and Bohemians, Lithuanians and Bulgars and Poles. That they went in such numbers is not surprising. The prestige of Italian teaching was great and well-established, whereas their own universities were few and scarcely more than nascent; indeed, when the Council of Vienne had ordained the teaching of Greek and other missionary languages in 1311, its injunctions went to France and Italy and England and Spain: but Germany had no university to which a missive could be directed. From Southern Germany, too, and Switzerland and Austria, the distance was small, notwithstanding the obvious Alps and the difficulties of the passes. Even Celtis, in spite of his denunciations, sent on his best pupils to Italy. So there were many who brought home with them to the North recollections of lofty condescension and of ill-disguised contempt for the foreigner: insults that they burned to repay.

Italy might vaunt the glories of ancient Rome; but Germany also had deeds to be proud of. Rome might have founded the World-empire; but Charlemagne had conquered the dominions of the Caesars and made the Empire Germanic. Classic antiquity, too, could not be denied to the land and people whom Tacitus had described; and Germans were not slow to claim the virtues found among them by the Roman historian. Arminius became the national hero. German faith and honour, German simplicity, German sincerity and candour—these are insisted upon by the Transalpine humanists with a vehemence which suggests that while priding themselves on the possession of such qualities, they marked the lack of them in others. We may recall Ascham's horror of the Englishman Italianated. Not that

Germans could not make friends in Italy. Scheurl loved his time at Bologna, and was eager to fight for the Bentivogli against Julius II. Erasmus was made much of by the Aldine Academy at Venice; and ten years later Hutten was charmed with his reception there. But with many, conscious of their own defects [1] and of the reality of Italian superiority, the charge of barbarism must have rankled. To Luther in 1518 Italian is synonymous with supercilious.

The rising German feeling expresses itself on all sides in the letters of the humanists. A young Frieslander, studying at Oxford in 1499, writes to a fellow-countryman there: 'Your verses have shown me what I never could have believed, that German talents are no whit inferior to Italian.' Hutten in 1516 writes of Reuchlin and Erasmus as 'the two eyes of Germany, whom we must sedulously cherish; for it is through them that our nation is ceasing to be barbarous'. Beatus Rhenanus, in editing the poems of Janus Pannonius (†1472), says in his preface, 1518: 'Janus and Erasmus, Germans though they are and moderns, give me as much satisfaction to read as do Politian and Hermolaus, or even Virgil and Cicero.' Erasmus in 1518 writes to thank a canon of Mainz who had entertained him at supper. After compliments on his host's charming manners, his erudition free from superciliousness—

[1] Thus a worthy abbot in the Inn valley, writing to Erasmus in 1523, manages to achieve a Latin letter, but apologizes for only being able to write in German characters.

if he could have known Gibbon, he surely must have used those immortal words of praise, 'a modest and learned ignorance'—and his wit and elegance of speech, he goes on: 'One might have been listening to a Roman. Now let the Italians go and taunt Germans with barbarism, if they dare!' In 1519 a canon of Brixen in Tirol writes to Beatus: 'Would to God that Germany had more men like you, to make her famous, and stand up against those Italians, who give themselves such airs about their learning; though men of credit now think that the helm has been snatched from their hands by Erasmus.' This is how Zwingli writes in 1521 of an Italian who had attacked Luther and charged him with ignorance: 'But we must make allowances for Italian conceit. In their heads is always running the refrain, "Heaven and earth can show none like to us". They cannot bear to see Germany outstripping them in learning.' Rarely a different note is heard, evoked by rivalry perhaps or the desire to encourage. Locher from Freiburg could call Leipzig barbarous. Erasmus wrote to an Erfurt schoolmaster that he was glad to see Germany softening under the influence of good learning and putting off her wild woodland ways. But these are exceptions: towards insolence from the South an unbroken front was preserved.

In another direction the strong national feeling manifested itself; in the study of German antiquity and the composition of histories.[1] Maximilian,

[1] Cf. A. Horawitz in Sybel's *Historische Zeitschrift*, xxv. (1871), 66–101; and P. Joachimsen, *Geschichtsauffassung und Geschicht-*

dipping his hands in literature, stimulated the archaeological researches of Peutinger, patronized Trithemius and Pirckheimer, and even instituted a royal historian, Stabius. Celtis the versatile projected an elaborate *Germania illustrata* on the model of Flavio Biondo's work for Rome; and his description of Nuremberg was designed to be the first instalment. As he conceived it, the work was never carried out; but essays of varying importance on this theme were produced by Cochlaeus, Pirckheimer, Aventinus and Munster. The most ardent to extol Germany was Wimpfeling of Schlettstadt, a man of serious temperament, who was prone to rush into controversy in defence of the causes that he had at heart. His education had all been got in Germany, and he was proud of his country. His first effort to increase its praise was to instigate Trithemius to put together a 'Catalogue of the illustrious men who adorn Germany with their talents and writings'. The author's preface (8 Feb. 1491) reveals unmistakably the animosity towards Italy: 'Some people contemn our country as barren, and maintain that few men of genius have flourished in it; hoping by disparagement of others to swell their own praise. With all the resources of their eloquence they trick out the slender achievements of their own countrymen; but jealousy blinds them to the great virtues of the Germans, the mighty deeds and brilliant intellects, the loyalty, enthusiasm and devotion of this

schreibung in Deutschland unter dem Einfluss des Humanismus, pt. 1, 1910.

great nation. If they find in the classics any credit given to us for valour or learning, they quickly hide it up ; and in order to trumpet their own excellences, they omit ours altogether. That is how Pliny's narrative of the German wars was lost, and how so many histories of our people have disappeared.'

The book was sent to Wimpfeling, who collected a few more names and added a preface of his own (17 Sept. 1492) in the same strain. 'People who think that Germany is still as barbarous as it was in the days of Caesar should read what Jerome has to say about it. The abundance of old books in existence shows that Germany had many learned men in the past ; who have left carefully written manuscripts on oratory, poetry, natural philosophy, theology and all kinds of erudition. All down the Rhine you will find the walls and roofs of monasteries adorned with elegant epigrams which testify to German taste of old. To-day there are Germans who can translate the Greek classics into Latin ; and if their style is not pure Ciceronian, let our detractors remember that styles change with the times. Mankind is always discontented, and prefers the old to the modern. I can quite understand that our German philosophers adapted their style to their audiences and their lofty subjects. So foreign critics had better let this provocative talk alone for ever.'

A few years later Wimpfeling edited a fourteenth-century treatise by Lupold of Bebenburg entitled 'The zeal and fervour of the ancient German princes towards the Christian religion and the servants of God'; the intention of which clearly fell in with his desire. In his preface, addressed to Dalberg, Agricola's patron, he tells a story which explains a peculiarity occasionally found in mediaeval manuscripts; of being written in sections by several different hands. Some years before, the Patriarch of Aquileia was passing through Spires. To divert the enforced leisure of a halt upon a journey, he prowled round the libraries of the town; and in one discovered this treatise of Lupold, which pleased him greatly. As he was to be off again next morning, there was no time to have it copied, at least by one hand: so the manuscript was cut up and distributed among a number of scribes, and in the space of a night the desired copy was ready. Subsequently Wimpfeling heard of the incident from one of the brethren in the monastery, and obtained the original manuscript to publish. When such things could happen, no wonder that some manuscripts are imperfect and others have disappeared.

Wimpfeling's next endeavour to assert the glories of Germany was completed in 1502; but did not appear till 1505. It was based upon the work of a friend, Sebastian Murrho of Colmar († 1494). The title, *Defensio Germaniae* or *Epithoma Germanorum*, sufficiently explains its purpose. After a brief account of Germany in Roman times—his hero being not Arminius, but 'the first German king, Arioviscus, who fought with Julius Caesar',—and fuller records of the Germanic Emperors since Charlemagne,

Wimpfeling comes to the praise of his own days; the men of learning, the famous soldiers, the architects who could build the great tower of Strasburg, the painters, the inventors of printing and of that terrible engine the bombard. But nearest to his heart lay a question debated then as now: to whom should rightfully belong the western part of the Rhine valley, between the river and the Vosges? It was there that his home lay, Schlettstadt, one of the fairest cities of the plain. With all the 'zeal and fervour of the ancient German princes' he sets out to prove that it must be German: 'where are there any traces' he cries 'of the French language? There are no books in French, no monuments, no letters, no epitaphs, no deeds or documents. For seven or eight centuries there is nothing but Latin or German.' The cathedral of Spires, the fine monastery of St. Fides in his native town, supply him with a further argument: would the good Dukes of Swabia have lavished so much money, the substance of their fathers, upon Gallic soil, to pour it out among the French? With such arguments he convinced himself and others. Almost at the same time Peutinger put out a little volume of 'Conversations about the wonderful antiquities of Germany'; supporting Wimpfeling with further evidence and concluding satisfactorily that French had never ruled over Germans.

A work of very different calibre which appeared about this time was the *Germaniae Exegesis* of Francis Fritz, who Latinized his name into Irenicus. Wimpfeling was growing grey when he had made his defence of Germany: the new champion was a young man of 23, who had scarcely emerged from his degree. The book was published in 1518; printed at Hagenau by Anshelm at the cost of John Koberger, the great Nuremberg printer, and fostered by Pirckheimer. In his later years Irenicus became a Lutheran and displayed some dignity in refusing to sacrifice his convictions to worldly interests; but at this time he was enthusiastic and heady, and as a result his work is an uncritical jumble. 'Puerile and silly' Erasmus called it, when he saw some of the proof-sheets at Spires in 1518. 'A most unfortunate book', wrote Beatus Rhenanus in 1525, 'without style and without judgement.' To Aventinus in 1531 it was 'an impudent compilation from Stabius and Trithemius, by a poor creature of the most despicable intelligence'. But even a bad book can be a measure of the time, showing the ideas current and the catchwords that were thought likely to attract the reading public. It is much larger than Wimpfeling's Defence, and even more miscellaneous; ranging over many aspects of Germany ancient and modern. To us in the present inquiry its interest lies in the frequency with which the excellence of Germany is asserted against Italian sneers. The following specimen will illustrate this point, and also explain Erasmus' epithets. In the chapter on the German language (ii. 30) Irenicus is throughout engaged in refuting the charge of German barbarism. 'It may be true', he says, 'that German is not so much declined as Latin: but complexity does not necessarily bring refinement. Germany is as rich in dialects as Italy, and to speak German well merits high praise. Italian may be directly descended from Latin; but German too has a considerable element of Latin and Greek words. Guarino and Petrarch have written poetry in their vernaculars, and so the Italians boast that their language is more suited to poetry. But more than 1000 years ago Ovid wrote a book of German poetry [1]; and Trebeta, son of Semiramis, is known to have been the first person to compose in German.'

In spite of such stuff, Pirckheimer, who saw the book in manuscript, was delighted with it. 'You have achieved what many have wished but few could have carried out. Every German must be obliged to you for the lustre you have brought to the Fatherland.' After stating that he had arranged with Koberger for the printing, he points out details which might be improved: more stress might be laid on the connexion of the Germans with the Goths, 'which the dregs of the Goths and Lombards—by which I mean the Italians—try to snatch from us'; and the universal conquests of the Goths might be more fully treated. Finally he suggests that before publication the work should be submitted to Stabius: 'the book deserves learned readers, and I should wish it to be as perfect as possible.' [2]

[1] Ovid, *Pont.* 4. 13. 19: Getico sermone.

[2] The letter is printed in Pirckheimer's *Opera*, 1610, p. 313: but is addressed wrongly, to Beatus Rhenanus.

This brief survey may close with a far more considerable work, the *Res Germanicae* of Beatus Rhenanus, published in 1531; from which we have made some extracts above. The book is sober and serious, and the subject-matter is handled scientifically; but in his preface Beatus is careful to point out that German history is as important as Roman, modern as much worth studying as ancient.

Such was the soil into which fell the seed that Luther went forth to sow. When Tetzel came marching into German towns, with the Pope's Bull borne before him on a cushion, and brandishing indulgences for the living and the dead, when the coins were tinkling in the box, and the souls, released by contract, were flying off out of purgatory, the religious sense of thinking men was outraged by this travesty of the Day of Judgement: but scarcely less were they angered to see the tinkling coins, honest German money, flying off as rapidly as the souls, to build palaces for the supercilious Italians. In the great struggle of the Reformation the main issue was of course religious; but even its leader could feel added bitterness in the knowledge that this shocking traffic was ordained from Italy to benefit an Italian Pope. If the sympathies of educated Germany had not already been strongly moved in the same direction, it is conceivable that Luther's intrepid protest might have lacked the support which carried it to success.

XI

ERASMUS AND THE BOHEMIAN BRETHREN

(A paper read before the third International Historical Congress, in London, April 1913.)

WHATEVER may still be the troubles of the great, amongst men of learning at any rate visits of ceremony are mercifully no longer in fashion. At first sight one is inclined to find the cause of this in an improved sense of the value of time. Modern inventions have taught first the business man and then the world in general that time is money. Improved communications with time-tables that may be relied upon enable us to arrange our days in such a way as to be at least more busy, if not more useful ; and we have acquired a wholesome respect for the time of others. But I do not think we should be right in accounting for the change in this way. At all ages the scholar, looking round him at tasks which exceed the capacity of a lifetime, has been avaricious of the hours—'labuntur anni', 'pereunt et imputantur' ever in his thoughts : and though the world of old moved slower, the man of business has rarely belied his name. A more plausible explanation is that the custom has died of surfeit. As increased facilities of travel made the world smaller, the circle of those that might be visited and saluted by the active grew boundless; so that on both sides limits were desired. Another consideration is that with new facilities came increased opportunities and hopes. To-day we live in the happy consciousness that friends, however distant, may be brought across the world to our doors by the urgencies of business or pleasure; and thus no one knows what the coming year may bring forth. In the sixteenth century men knew that opportunities lost might never recur, and that they must seize or make them as best they might.

At that time visits of ceremony were in great vogue. Officials and scholars alike groaned under them. After a visit to the Court Erasmus writes: 'If Pollio (a disguised name, as he was writing of a man who afterwards became an intimate friend) has been with you, you will understand what I suffered at Brussels; every day hosts of Spanish visitors, besides Italians and Germans.' A little later he apologizes to a correspondent for having given him a chilly welcome: 'just then I had escaped from Brussels, quite worn out with the salutations of these persistent Spaniards.' The custom was widespread. An English graduate, studying for a time at Louvain, congratulates himself on having escaped from it at Cambridge. Clenardus found it thriving at Salamanca; Casaubon complained of it at Montpellier; in Oxford it was even obligatory for intending disputants in the schools to pay formal visits beforehand to their examiners.

In 1517 Erasmus' fame was at its zenith; and in

consequence visitors came to him from every side, some to seek counsel, others to adore. His correspondence gives us many instances. In the spring of 1517, when the Cardinal of Gurk attended Maximilian to the Netherlands, his two secretaries, Richard Bartholinus of Perugia and Ursinus Velius, a Silesian, prepared panegyrical verses with which to greet Erasmus if they should have the good fortune to meet him. For some reason Bartholinus alone came, and, presenting both the poems, elicited a complimentary letter in reply. A more distinguished visitor received less attention. In the summer of 1518 Erasmus was at Basle, printing the notes to his second edition of the New Testament. The Bishop of Pistoia, nephew of one of the most influential cardinals, and Papal nuncio in Switzerland, also came to Basle. Wishing to see the great scholar, he asked him to dinner. But Erasmus could not spare the time. He declined, and in his place sent his friends, Beatus Rhenanus and the young Amerbachs. Three times he made excuse; and at length the Nuncio went on foot to seek in Froben's press the scholar who would not come to him. What their conversation was we do not know; but before leaving, the Nuncio ordered a copy of the Amerbach–Froben Jerome to be sent to the binders and equipped with his arms and adornments.

Later in the year the enthusiastic Eobanus of Hesse appeared in Louvain. He had come from Erfurt where he was teaching, and the main purpose of his journey was to see Erasmus. His *Hodoeporicon*, printed on his return, describes his course in detail. With a young companion, John Werter, also from Erfurt, he entered Louvain in the evening. Next morning early they sent in their 'callow' verses to the great man, and followed shortly themselves. Erasmus came down to greet them at the door with a kindly welcome, and Eobanus describes a banquet to which he invited them, entertaining them with serious talk and light-hearted jest. But it was at no light cost to Erasmus' time: for when his admirers left five days later, he had been cajoled into writing six letters of compliment, two to the travellers themselves and four more to friends at Gotha and Erfurt. But this was not the only cost. Eobanus imbued others of the Erfurt circle with his hero-worship; and next year came two more, Jonas and Schalbe, to trouble Erasmus' leisure, when he was taking a spring holiday at Antwerp, 'by the sea', and to bear off more letters to Erfurt. The spirit that animated these visitors is shown in a letter of John Turzo, bishop of Breslau, a man of Erasmus' own age. In 1518 Ursinus Velius, the disappointed secretary of the Cardinal of Gurk, had become canon of Breslau on Turzo's presentation; and had doubtless talked to his patron of Erasmus' attractive gifts. 'I am most eager to visit you' wrote the Bishop, from Breslau. 'If ever I had heard that you were anywhere within a week's journey from here, I should have rushed over at once: indeed I would have gone as far as Belgium, if only the business of my office allowed. The men of Cadiz who journeyed to Rome to see Livy were not more eager.'

A picture of the interruptions to which Erasmus was exposed is given in a preface written in Froben's name for the new edition of Erasmus' *Epigrammata* combined with More's and with the *Utopia*, March 1518. 'Most of these verses' Froben is made to say 'were written not for publication, but to give pleasure to friends; to whom he is always very obliging. When he was here bringing out his New Testament and Jerome, heavens! how he worked! toiling away untiringly day after day. Never was any one more overwhelmed in composition; and yet certain great persons thought themselves entitled to come and waste his time, coaxing out of him a few lines of verse or a little letter. So compliant was he that they made it very difficult for him. To refuse seemed uncivil when they pressed him so. But to write when his mind was intent elsewhere, and not a minute to spare from his labours——! However, he did write, on the spur of the moment, turning aside for a little to the groves of the Muses.'

Some other visitors can be traced in this period. John Alexander Brassicanus, poet laureate, came from Tubingen in September 1520 and saw Erasmus at Antwerp; whence in reply to a letter of self-introduction he bore away a complimentary letter that he afterwards printed, and the sound piece of advice, that if he wished to become learned, he must never think himself so. More distinguished was Ferdinand Columbus, the explorer's natural son and heir, who in October 1520, on one of those journeys on which he gathered his famous library, received at Louvain a copy of Erasmus' *Antibarbari*, with his name inscribed in it by the author. A visitor to whom we must pay more heed was John Draco, one of the Erfurt circle, who in July 1520 came to pay homage at Louvain.

In the autumn of 1518 the agent of a Leipzig bookseller trading to Prague received a letter to carry back with him and forward on to Erasmus at Louvain. The writer was a certain Jan Slechta, a Bohemian country gentleman, who was living at Kosteletz on the upper waters of the Elbe, a few miles to the North-east of Prague. He was a man of education and position. After taking his M.A. at Prague in 1484, he had served for sixteen years as a secretary to King Ladislas of Bohemia and Hungary; but about 1507, disgusted with the turmoils of court life in that very troubled time, he had retired to his home, to give his later years to the education of his son and the personal management of his estates. The world of affairs had not extinguished his love of learning. He was an intimate friend of Bohuslaus of Hassenstein, scholar and traveller, and corresponded with him in elegant Latin. Attracted by the reputation for eloquence won by the notorious Hieronymus Balbus, he had persuaded him *c.* 1499 to come and teach in Prague—a step which in view of Balbus' bad life he afterwards deeply regretted. He was also the author of a dialogue on the relations of body and soul, entitled *Microcosmus*; which with characteristic modesty he kept for more than twenty years known only to his intimate friends—indeed it was only in the last year of his life that he composed a dedication for it, and it seems never to have been printed.

The tone of Slechta's thoughts in his later years was grave and serious ; as well it might be. The two kingdoms, then but loosely united, were torn with internal factions and racial jealousies ; while in church towers and over city gates the bells hung ready to proclaim to the countryside the advent of that ever-present menace, the Turk. In the priesthood men could mark much that was amiss ; and the seamless robe of Christ was rent with schism, the candle that Hus and Jerome had lighted a century before, still burning clearly among less sober heresies, which drew down on it, as upon themselves, spasmodic outbursts of retributive violence. Uneasy sat the crown on Ladislas' head ; and when Death, coming as a friend, took it from him in 1516, it was only to thrust this sad office upon a ten-year-old boy, who after ten more years of childish government was miserably to perish at Mohacz. No wonder that Slechta and his friends looked anxiously upon the future. 'The times of Hus and Wycliffe which our grandfathers detested, seem golden beside our own' wrote Bohuslaus to Geiler of Kaisersberg—a member of that grave circle of Strasburg humanists, with which, it may be noted in passing, our Bohemians had much in common. The letters of Slechta contain two disquisitions, one on the frailties of a celibate clergy, the other on the duties of a parish priest; advocating reforms by which he hoped to check the continuous growth of 'those unutterable heretics, the Pyghards': by whom he meant the Bohemian Brethren.

What moved Slechta to correspond with Erasmus we do not know; possibly a slighting reference in one of the latter's printed letters to 'those schismatic Bohemians, who have infected most of Europe'. Slechta's letter is unhappily lost; but from Erasmus' reply, dated 23 April 1519 from Louvain, its general tenor may be gathered. It began, of course, with eulogies of Erasmus and his work; and then, after some account of the writer's life and fortunes, it proceeded to assure him that there were persons in Bohemia who were not merely interested in good learning but prepared to advance it. Finally it invited him to come to Prague. Erasmus' answer to his unknown correspondent was courteous, but firmly declined the invitation. 'What I can do at Prague I do not see. It is considerate of you to offer me an escort for my journey; but I confess I do not like regions where such company is necessary. In this country one can go about wherever one likes, alone. I am sure that, as you say, I should find among you plenty of learned and pious men, who are not contaminated with the errors of schism. But how is it that this division is suffered to remain? Better unity with some hardship than to hold one's own at the cost of discord. I fear it is money that stands in the way. Paul suffered the loss of all things that he might win Christ. The world is full of cardinals and princes and bishops ; if only one of these would take up this matter in a truly Christian spirit ! If Paul were on the Pope's throne, I am sure he would allow not only his revenues but his authority to be diminished, if his loss would purchase unity.' Erasmus concludes cordially : 'If we cannot meet, at any rate we can write. I will walk and talk with you sometimes beside your Elbe, you shall come and dwell with me in Brabant. Friendship can flourish without actual contact.'

This letter was handed to Slechta on 11 September, four and a half months after it was written. Nearly a year had elapsed since his letter had been dispatched and he had given up hopes of a reply : so that these amiable and encouraging words were the more welcome, and he at once proceeded to act upon them. Within a month he had composed a letter of some elegance, in which while subscribing to Erasmus' prayers for unity, he pointed out the difficulties of the task. To the remarks about coming to Prague he rejoined regretfully : 'I can quite see that there is nothing for you to do here. There are many of us who would have been glad of your coming ; but I understand that we must hope to see you at another time and elsewhere. That travellers in our country need an escort you would not wonder if you could see how the roads run, among lofty mountains shrouded in impenetrable forests. These give cover to hordes of brigands, who prey upon travellers and merchants, robbing and killing indifferently. Almost every month there are punitive raids made from the towns, and brigands are captured and put to death. But the pest seems ineradicable.'

Slechta then proceeds to the religious troubles, and after expressing general agreement with Erasmus, describes the three main parties into which the life of Bohemia and Moravia was cloven. First the orthodox Romanists, loyal to the Church and in unity with Germany and the rest of Christendom ; finding their adherents amongst the upper classes, together with some of the King's cities and the monasteries, many of which, though once rich, had now fallen into decay. Secondly, the Utraquists, otherwise orthodox but practising communion in both kinds, and at their services reading the Epistle and Gospel in the vernacular : with some supporters among the nobility, a good many gentry, and nearly thirty royal cities. After tracing their history from the Council of Basle and briefly stating their views, he adds that no one in the kingdom is able to propound a solution of the difficulties existing. Thirdly, the Bohemian Brethren, whom he styles Pyghards. This name, from the opprobrious sense in which it is generally used, is now thought to be derived from the Beghards, a mediaeval sect whose vagaries drew down upon it frequent persecution ; but Slechta traces it to a foreign vagabond who came from Picardy in 1422 and infected with his pestilent doctrines the army of John Ziska, the Taborite, an army of those that were in distress, in debt, in discontent.

This sect, Slechta tells us, lasted continuously

down to the times of the late King Ladislas († 1516), and indeed increased considerably under him ; for his thoughts were much occupied with Hungary, and he was content if Bohemia could be maintained in an outward appearance of peace. Then follows a description of their opinions. 'The Pope and all his officials they regard as Antichrist. They choose their own bishops, rude unlettered laymen, with wives and families. They salute one another as Brother and Sister ; and recognize no authority but the Bible. Their priests celebrate mass without vestments, use leavened bread and only the Lord's Prayer. Transubstantiation they deny, and the worship of the host they regard as idolatry. Vows to the saints, prayers for the dead, and confession to priests they ridicule ; and they keep no holy days but Sundays, Christmas, Easter and Whitsun.' 'I will not waste your time with more of these pernicious views. My feeling is that if the two first-named parties could only be reconciled, this nefarious sect might, with the aid of the King, be exterminated or at any rate reduced to a better state of faith and religion.'

The roads in Bohemia might be dangerous, but the distance to Louvain was not so great as it had seemed at first ; for Erasmus' reply is dated 1 Nov. 1519, only three weeks after Slechta's letter. He begins again with the roads. 'Prevention is better than punishment. It would be wiser if, instead of these avenging raids, the more frequented roads could be cleared of forest on either side, and held by blockhouses and armed posts at intervals. Indeed it is somewhat discreditable that the great towns and princes of Germany cannot achieve what the Swiss do by co-operation and local action.' He then turns to the religious dissensions, and in his passion for concord exclaims that it would be better that a nation should be united in error than so numerously divided: experience shows that there is no opinion so wild but that some one will be found to embrace it. Of the orthodox party he has nothing to say beyond extolling the system by which the Pope might act as judge and father of all, and as supreme court of appeal. To the Utraquists he would counsel conformity to the practice of the majority; although unable to understand why the Church should have allowed a practice instituted by Christ to fall into disuse.

Then he comes to the Brethren, and after admitting that they have strayed further than the Utraquists from the rule of Christian life, he continues: 'If they go on still in their wickedness, they must be restrained; but this is not the duty of any one who likes, nor must violence be used, lest the innocent suffer with the guilty. Their practice of electing their own priests and bishops has authority in antiquity; but it certainly is unfortunate if their choice falls on men bad as well as unlearned. With the titles of Brother and Sister I see no fault to find: it is a pity they are not more widely used among Christians. To prefer God's word in the Bible to the judgements of Doctors is sound: though to reject the latter altogether is as uniform an error as to embrace them to the exclusion of everything else. To celebrate the mass in everyday dress is not contrary to the truth ; but it is a pity to abandon customs sanctioned by use and authority : though perhaps the Pope might be persuaded to concede to them the use of their own rites, as he does to the Greeks and the Milanese. The Lord's Prayer is, of course, part of our own use ; and though it seems narrow to confine themselves to this, I doubt whether they do worse than those who weave in long strings of intercession from any source. Their opinions about the sacraments are certainly impious; but at any rate they are under no temptation to exploit these holy mysteries for the sake of gain or futile glory or tyrannous imposition. I do not see why they should reject vigils and fasts in moderation ; but these are matters for encouragement rather than positive command. About festivals they seem to follow the usage current in the days of Jerome : better, I think, than the modern calendar, full of saints-days which end in riot and carouse, and on which the honest journeyman is forbidden to work for his children's bread.' As Slechta read these words, he must surely have felt as did Balak, the son of Zippor, when he listened to the seer from Mesopotamia taking up his parable upon Israel in the plains of Moab. The man whose eyes were open, had blessed the Brethren instead of cursing them ; and literary Europe might well follow his lead.

The history of the Bohemian Brethren is of exceptional interest, affording an example of a community professing a plain, simple faith and ruling their lives by modest conceptions of ordinary goodness, who, guided by leaders almost unknown to the world, through the trials of good and evil repute, through tribulation and prosperity, kept serenely upon the path they had marked out for themselves, living and growing into one of the most flourishing and devoted missionary bodies of the present day. As is natural under such conditions, their origin is not free from obscurity. Men connected them with the Waldensians of Southern France, or traced them, as we have seen, to a leader from Picardy. Through the fifteenth century they grew steadily in strength and unity, sheltered by the toleration which Rome unwillingly granted to the Utraquists as a result of the Compacts of Basle; and as compared with other dissentient bodies their name was singularly free from gross imputations. Throughout that age such imputations were freely made and believed against heretics. This was not unreasonable. In the low state of public and private morals faith was regarded as an indispensable bulwark to conduct, the faith which taught indeed that a man should love God and his neighbour, but stablished him into practising what he professed, by lurid pictures of the fate awaiting him if he did not. Without this bulwark it was not thought possible that a man could lead a godly, righteous and sober life; and so he was considered capable of every form of vice, if he ventured to doubt the truth of those opinions on which the Church had set its seal, in realms into which it now seems that human knowledge cannot penetrate.

At the beginning of the sixteenth century fresh

attempts were being made to win back the Brethren to orthodoxy; and in this work the ardour of the Dominicans burned bright. In 1500 one of them, Henry Institor, a Doctor of Theology, procured from Alexander VI bulls which recognized him as 'Inquisitor into heresy throughout Germany and Bohemia', and empowered him to collect heretical books and send them to the Bishop of Olmutz, the chief see of Moravia, to be burned; also to join to himself two or three other Masters of Theology and preach against the heretics. These bulls are printed at the head of a great volume written by Institor, with the title 'A shield for the faith of the Holy Roman Church against the heresy of the Waldensians or Pickards, who on all sides are infecting with virulent contagion certain races in Germany and Bohemia, to hatred of the clergy and enervation of the ecclesiastical power'. In 1501 the volume appeared at Olmutz, with an enumeration of thirty-six erroneous articles in which the Pickards denied the authority of the Church; followed of course by a vigorous refutation. At the same time one of their own countrymen, Augustine Kasenbrot of Olmutz was writing a series of open letters on the Brethren and their views.

But the most succinct account of the position is contained in an attack made upon them by a learned and fair-minded Dominican, Jacobus Lilienstayn. His book, 'a Treatise against the erroneous Waldensian Brethren, commonly known as the Pickards, without rule, without law, and without obedience, of whom there are many in Moravia, more than in

Bohemia', was composed in 1505 and is dedicated to the Dean of Prague. It begins by setting forth five general and twelve special errors of the Waldensians. The former are as follows:

1. They call the Gospels, the Epistles and the Acts, together with the Old Testament where it agrees with the New, 'the Law of Christ'; and they attack and deride the Doctors of the Church.
2. They say the Pope has no more power in administering the sacraments of the Church, and in other ecclesiastical matters, than a simple priest has.
3. They say that in the practice of the Church nothing is to be added to what Christ and the Apostles taught and did.
4. They hold the pure text of the Gospel without any gloss.
5. They allege that the Church is in error, and that they themselves are the brethren of Christ and the true imitators of the Apostles.

Amongst the special errors are denials of the validity of indulgences and of the efficacy of masses for the dead; and the general simplicity of their conduct is shown in their practices at birth and death, baptism requiring only pure water, not holy oil and the chrism, and extreme unction banished from the death-bed.

Finally the good Dominican gives a brief account of the life of these Brethren 'without obedience'. In his preface he expresses his difficulty in gathering the truth about them: 'for they are as inconstant as the moon, and the practices alleged against them in the past are denied by them to-day.' But he concludes honestly that though their faith is 'abhominable' to true Christians, their life is good enough. His good sense is further shown by his refusal to accept an absurd story about their method of choosing their leaders. 'When one of these is to be chosen', so ran the tale, 'the community meets together. And as they sit in silence, the windows being open, a great fly enters and buzzes over them, settling at length on the head of one; who is then set apart for a season. And when he is brought back, he is found to be learned in Latin and theology and whatever else is necessary, though he were rude and ignorant before.' This Lilienstayn finds clearly false: the simple life of the Brethren he illustrates by their practice. 'They have Bibles in Bohemian, which they read. Their women wear veils, and no colours, only black, white and grey. They all labour with their hands.' Thus their life to him was 'good enough'. It may remind us in many points of the Quakers.

The attacks upon them led the Brethren to reply. In 1507 they composed an *Apologia* addressed to the King, to show that they were not without rule, without law and without obedience, and to defend the manner of their life. This was printed at Nuremberg in 1507, and again in 1518; but of the original editions I have not been able to see a copy. The attacks continued. In 1512 another ponderous volume appeared, composed by Jacob Ziegler, the well-known Bavarian scientist, to demonstrate the falsity of their opinions. What finally impelled the Brethren to court countenance from Erasmus is not clear ; possibly the cool reception the Utraquists had had from Luther the year before, with the rather contemptuous suggestion that their style and opinions were more like Erasmus' than his own. The episode has escaped Erasmus' biographers ; and I cannot find any mention of it except an allusion in one of his letters, and a description in a treatise on the Brethren by Joachim Camerarius the elder (1500–1574). Camerarius' book was not published till 1605 ; but we can perhaps trace the source of his information. From 1518 onwards he spent some years at Erfurt. In January 1521 Erasmus describes the visit of the Brethren's envoys as having occurred six months before ; at Antwerp, according to Camerarius, where he may be traced in June 1520. If we recall that it was in July that Draco came from Erfurt to pay his visit of homage, it seems quite likely that on his return he may have given to Camerarius the detailed record which the latter has preserved.

By that time Erasmus' name was well known in Central Europe. 'Both from Hungary and Bohemia' he says in 1518 'bishops and men of position write to thank me for my New Testament.' Apart from the learned world there were others, too, who must have known him ; for a Bohemian translation had just appeared of the new preface to his *Enchiridion*, a preface in which he had written with an almost

Lutheran freedom about abuses in the Church, and had extolled the life of simple Christianity. This was a book to appeal at once to the Brethren. Another of his works which may have had its effect in attracting them was the *Julius Exclusus*. This exquisitely witty satire dealt freely with the Pope and his office, the Pope whom the Brethren accounted no more than a simple priest; and though its licence was too bold for Erasmus ever to admit its authorship—indeed, as we have seen, he consistently denied it—, it was attributed to him on all sides, in company with others, his secret being on the whole well kept. The *Julius* was translated into Bohemian, somewhere about this time: but from the nature of it, a kind of book to which publishers as well as authors were loath to put their names, it cannot be definitely placed. So it was, too, with the *Moria*, which had been translated by Gregory Hruby Gelenski, father of the scholar, Sigismund Gelenius; but of which no contemporary edition survives.

If the Brethren had seen Erasmus' final letter to Slechta, they might well have been encouraged to hope much from him. But of this there is no indication. Slechta was hardly likely to communicate it to them; and though such documents often leaked out against the owner's will, its first appearance in print was in 1521, in Erasmus' *Epistolae ad diuersos*. I cannot find any translation into a vernacular except a German version by John Froben of Andernach which appeared at Nuremberg in 1531.

Whatever was the motive attraction, the Brethren

sent as their envoys, so Camerarius tells us, Nicholas Claudianus, a learned physician, and Laurence Voticius (Woticky), a man of many accomplishments, who died at a good age in 1565—a date, which, if it be not a later interpolation, is an indication as to when Camerarius composed his narrative.[1] They brought with them a copy of their *Apologia*, printed at Nuremberg in 1511—a date which appears to be wrong—and presented it to Erasmus at Antwerp with the request that he would read it through and see if there was anything in it that he would wish to have changed. If that were so, they would readily defer to his criticisms; but if, as they hoped, he approved of what they said, it would be a help and consolation to them if he would express that opinion.

He took the book and said he would be glad to read it; but when after a few days they came for his answer, he told them he had been too busy to do more than glance through it: so far as he had gone, he found no error and nothing that he would wish to alter. He declined, however, to bear testimony about it, as this would bring them no help, and only danger to himself. 'You must not think', he said, 'that any words of mine will bring you support; indeed, my own influence, such as it is, requires the backing of others. If it is true that my writings are of any value to divine and useful learning, it seems to me unwise to jeopardize their influence by proclaiming publicly the agreement between us: such actions

[1] L. Camerarius, in his preface, 1 Jan. 1605, describes the book as composed 'more than thirty years ago'.

might lead to their being condemned and torn from the hands of the public. Forgive me for this caution, you will perhaps call it fear: and be assured that I wish you well and will most gladly help you in other matters.' The envoys were disappointed, Camerarius records, but took his refusal in good part: for they relied not on the judgements of men to be the foundation of their heavenly edifice of truth. The good sense of his words no doubt appealed to them; for the Brethren were above all things moderate men, averse from violence, convinced perhaps by their own experience that a display of courage is unwise when it provokes opposition and raises obstacles to progress.

The matter was not, however, allowed to rest. In the same year an appeal on behalf of the Brethren was made to Erasmus from another quarter. One of the features of their movement had been the number of the nobility who had become sympathizers, if not actual members of the community. One of these was Artlebus of Boskowitz, a kinsman perhaps of that 'nobilis virgo, Martha de Boskowitz' whom the Brethren in addressing the King had adduced as one of their supporters. From the castle of Znaim, his official residence as Supreme Captain of Moravia, Artlebus wrote, telling Erasmus of the steady growth of the Brethren, and of the futility of all attempts to withstand their doctrines by argument; and sending him a copy of their Rule, with the request that he would read it and frame thereupon a standard of Christian piety, which all men, including the Brethren, might follow. He turned then to praise Luther for the courageous fight he was making, and urged Erasmus to join with him in sowing the seed of the Gospel.

Erasmus' reply, dated 28 Jan. 1521 from Louvain, has no address but 'N. viro praepotenti'; and in consequence its connexion with Artlebus of Boskowitz has escaped notice. As was to be expected, he declined the proposal that he should set up a standard of Christian observance. He might criticize with all freedom the practices of monks and clergy and speak straightly of Papal iniquities: but the standard of the Church was still the life of Christ, and he would not arrogate to himself the right to draw the picture of this anew. He took the opportunity to lament, as he had done to Slechta, the discord prevailing in Bohemia, and to urge that a serious attempt should be made to reconcile the Brethren to the Church. But since his correspondence with Slechta the world had gone forward. Luther had burned the Pope's bull at Wittenberg, and Aleander at Worms was pressing the Diet to annihilate him. Erasmus has less to say to Artlebus in favour of the Brethren than he had said to Slechta: indeed, after the appeal for moderation, he goes no further than to condemn the attitude of the opponents of the Papacy, doubtless intending to include among them the Brethren. About Luther he would give no decided opinion. 'It is absurd how men condemn Luther's books without reading them. Some parts of Luther's writings are good; but parts are not, and over these I skip. If Luther stands by the Catholic Church, I will gladly join him.' Artlebus' reply is not extant; but a sentence in a letter of Erasmus to Wolsey a year later shows that the 'Bohemian Captain' was greatly vexed by the failure of his overtures.

This is the last trace of Erasmus' correspondence with Bohemia. But, uncompromising as he had been in his refusal to both appeals, his influence there was only just at its commencement, if we may judge by the list of his works translated into Bohemian, which the Ghent bibliography has brought to light. The translation of his preface to the *Enchiridion* was followed by his version of the *Saturnalia* of Lucian (first published in 1517) in 1520; the *Precatio dominica* (1523) in 1526; his version of the New Testament in 1533; some of the Colloquies in 1534; the *De Ciuilitate* (1530) in 1537; the Paraphrase on St. Matthew (1522) and the *De puritate Ecclesiae* (1536) in 1542; the *De immensa Dei misericordia* (1524) in 1558 and 1573; the *Apophthegmata Graeciae sapientum* (1514) in 12 editions between 1558 and 1599; the *De praeparatione ad mortem* (1534) in 1564 and 1786; and the *Vidua Christiana* (1529) in 1595. The envoys of the Brethren were perhaps wise enough to see that they had much to learn from the man who was courageous enough to preach caution and to let himself appear afraid.

INDEX